Daddy Gear

(Everything I Wish I'd Known about Becoming a Dad)

Jed Gibson

For my brother, may fatherhood bring you all the joys it has brought me.

"Why just do it, when you can overdo it?"
-Gibson Family motto

Table of Contents

About the Author

Introduction

When I was learning to make crème brulée, the five-star chef/author of the cookbook I was using said his favorite way to caramelize the sugar was to use a salamander. That was excellent advice. The only problem was that I had no idea what a salamander was unless it was pulled out of a stream. What does this have to do with becoming a dad for the first time? Every trade has its tools. And the tools in those trades have names you may not understand. Becoming a parent is no different. Think glider, or Bjorn, or Puckie.

This book started out as a simple list for my brother explaining to him the different stuff he'd need to get ready for his first child. There's plenty written about what to expect when you're expecting: what she's going through, what you're going through, how to be a good parent, how to remain macho, or hip, or cool. What I couldn't find, and the reason I wrote this list for my brother, was a book that explained all the stuff I'd need and gave me some insight into all the things no one ever tells you.

The book is, for the most part, about things, large and small: diapers and bottles and spoons and also backpacks and cribs and minivans. As I began compiling the list I realized that not only did things need an explanation or description, but there were also countless lessons we'd learned along the way that I wanted to pass along. There is so much to know about the physical stuff you need when you have a child. For every "thing" you need for your house, car, or baby there are multiple options, colors and qualities. Although many, if not most, salespeople know their product, I find myself wary of their opinions because they're, well, salespeople and they want to sell me their stuff. So I felt it was my brotherly duty to pass along advice that was not biased toward a particular brand.

As I wrote I realized there were also so many lessons I wanted to pass along about how to get ready for their baby, like what to expect in the hospital, how to find a pediatrician, and why you should really get a dog, that my list slowly grew into something more. Add to that the many situations where my wife and I found ourselves scratching our heads and wondering, "how come no one ever told us that?" so I wanted to pass that along too.

Let me explain something about the family I grew up with. We're technophiles, all of us. We research any product we buy to the point of being absurd. We save the owner's manuals to all of it. We're what you might call power users. We love toys, tools, all forms of intricate programmable electronic stuff. I rebuild computers, remodel houses, rebuild carburetors (20 years ago), and am a recovering hacker. We always read the instructions (thanks, Dad.) We know what every button on our gadgets does and we're not afraid to tinker. For example, my dad took apart the state-of-the-art Lutron programmable lighting control system in his house and soldered in new parts so it works on a timer. Get the picture?

My wife, Sandy, on the other hand comes from a family of "on-off" people. That's right, Sandy doesn't care what all the buttons do. "How do I turn it on and turn it off?" That's what's important to her. She's also a safety freak, which isn't a bad thing. The two of us make an interesting dichotomy. In addition to researching what works and making sure it satisfies my needs, I also have to make sure it's easy to use. All this means we have a very well-equipped, safe home. In this book I have tried to point out the areas where I went overboard on gadgetry, so you won't make the same mistake.

So now I have my own family: two girls and a boy. We've gotten through having a baby three times. At press time they were nine, seven, and five and no longer babies. But when I sat down and started writing the first draft of this book our daughter Sidney was almost two and we were pregnant with our second child, our daughter Ellie. Our boy, Calvin, followed surprisingly soon after Ellie. If you're wondering about the time lag between the first draft and publication, it's called parenthood and I love every minute of it.

I've organized the book into three basic sections. The first is about getting prepared. What books to read, what books she'll probably read, and my perspective on some of the courses we took. The second part is all about the stuff you'll be getting. Believe me, there's a lot of it. It really surprised me how many different types of things we ended up with. Lastly, there are some life lessons and commentary about what to expect as a first-time dad. In the end, you have to relax and live it, but hopefully what follows will talk you down from the ledge and be helpful.

A note about wives versus partners, surrogates, etc. Because I am in a "traditional" marriage my notes often refer to my wife, who is my partner and friend. But much of the advice in this book is equally relevant whether you are a single parent or in a same-sex relationship.

Jed Gibson

Section 1 – Preparation

Having a baby, the first time, is a mystery. At least it was to me. I remember asking a friend how he felt when he and his wife had their first baby. He told me that aside from being excited, he had a general apprehension about the unknown. That pretty much summed it up. So before you go out and start accumulating "stuff" you may want to take a few minutes to do some prep work. I've outlined some of the things you should know and do long before Baby arrives.

Chapter One - The First Decisions

Doctor or Midwife

You may think that the first decision you make is whether or not to have a baby. I disagree. Although we planned on starting a family, some people just have a "surprise." Either way, before, or slightly after you get pregnant you have to decide what kind of medical care you want to get. Your main choices are a doctor or a midwife, but you may also want a home birth. This is totally a personal choice and one I would venture to say is 99% up to your wife. Sandy wanted a midwife because she felt the care was more personal and the midwife would spend more time in the delivery room "laboring" with us. To be clear, midwives are degreed professionals with intimate medical knowledge. My mother-in-law firmly believed they performed some type of home birth voodoo, but after coming to a few appointments and being present at one of the births she came around. The reason we shied away from using a doctor is that from what I've read, many doctors don't spend that much time with you in the delivery room. They come in when just before delivery and "catch" the baby.

One other note about practices: many group practices with multiple doctors or midwives don't let you pick who is actually going to deliver your baby. It all comes down to who's on call when your wife goes into labor. You, therefore, have no say over who, specifically, will be delivering your baby. So it's a good idea to meet all the people in the practice. You may be able to better predict who will be with you if you use a sole practitioner, but if your doctor or midwife is away on vacation, you'll get whoever is covering for them. Which means you may meet the person delivering your baby for the first time at the hospital.

Is it a Boy or a Girl?

Finding out whether you're having a boy or a girl is one of the joys of modern science. Knowing the gender can help you plan the nursery, buy clothes, and determine the theme of things to come. Many, if not most, of the people we know wanted to know in advance the gender of their baby. We emphatically did not.

If you decide you do not want to know whether you're having a boy or a girl understand you are going against what has become the cultural norm in this country. We were pressured by virtually every member of our family, each time we were pregnant. There is also the practical concern that medical staff is accustomed to telling you the gender. So be warned. You have to tell the sonogram technicians, at every appointment, that you don't want to know the gender. You have to tell your doctor or midwife, the hospital staff, and everyone on the medical staff. Wearing a sign around your neck might not be too subtle. At the end of the day, we loved the surprise and were overjoyed to have healthy babies with ten fingers and ten toes.

Chapter Two - Required Reading

There is a cliché that there's no substitute for experience. Having a baby is no exception. There is nothing that can prepare you in advance for a new experience. You have to go through it to truly understand it. However, doing some research in advance can go a long way toward easing your anxiety about the mysteries of childbirth. The reading list below helped me see what others experienced, and relate to and get closer to my wife as we went through our first pregnancy. It also helped both of us keep Sidney, our first born, alive when we got home from the hospital.

What to Expect When You're Expecting, Eisenberg, Murkoff and Hathaway, Workman Publishing, 2008

This is a staple for women everywhere and is probably one of the best selling books of all time. It goes into great detail about the changes she's going through both medically and emotionally. My wife read it religiously when she was pregnant with Sidney. I have to admit I didn't spend all that much time with it. However, you can get points with your wife if you buy it for her when you start "trying."

A Girlfriends Guide to Pregnancy, Iovine, Perigee, Simon and Schuster, 2007
This non-technical, no-nonsense guide tells it like it is, woman to woman. So if you're not actually having the baby, it may not be for you. However, your wife will love it. Sandy found this book to be funny and reassuring at the same time. It imparted valuable information with a humorous spin on things so she didn't feel like she was losing her mind.

Your Pregnancy Week by Week, Curtis and Schuler, Fisher Books, 2007
With our first baby, my wife and I would spend some time together each week reading the chapter that covered the upcoming week. It was nice to share what was going on in her body. As our pregnancy progressed and the chapters got longer, there was more and more information on birth defects and disorders. Unless you're sure you need to know, I'd avoid this stuff. You can drive yourself nuts worrying about the health of your unborn child. If you've had all the tests

your doctor recommends, and know the baby is healthy, there's no need for the added stress of "what ifs." With subsequent kids we didn't spend as much time reading the book, which epitomized an issue that many people face with multiple kids. You get so wrapped up in what's going on with the first. But with subsequent kids a lot of it is second nature.

Womanly Art of Breastfeeding, Wiessinger, West and Pitman, Ballentine Books, 2010

This book is definitely not geared toward guys. No, there are no hot pictures of naked women. It covers a plethora of information about breastfeeding. Apparently it's not as simple as you might think. I found it a valuable resource when we were trying to figure out how long we could store breast milk in various states, refrigerated and frozen, and how long I could keep a bottle out without worrying about the milk going bad.

Baby Name Books

There are dozens of these so you may find yourself with several. In addition to the name, many books give you definitions of the name's meaning. As is typical with having multiple children we were able to relax and spend a quiet evening by the fire picking out names for the first, got completely overwhelmed and ran out of time with our second, but for the third child we were able to again carve out some time by the fire after the others were in bed. In other words, we were getting the hang of juggling children and pregnancy. One thing you may want to consider is checking the Social Security website:

(www.ssa.gov/OACT/babynames) to see what the current "most popular" names are in case you don't want your child to be one of 50 Madisons in her grade.

It's a Baby not Just a Pregnancy

So then one day we realized we'd spent all this time getting ready to have a baby. We'd read everything we could find, gone to parenting classes, taken infant CPR, built a beautiful nursery, but we had no idea what to do when we brought the baby home. Perhaps this is a slight exaggeration. The parenting class did teach us how to give Sidney a bath. Anyway, this realization was scary. What to do with a new child? What else, more reading. The three books below we found extremely helpful:

What to Expect in the First Year, Murkoff, Workman Publishing, 2008

This book was invaluable with our first child when we were trying to figure out what's "normal." For example, at what age range should we expect Sidney to sit up without help, or roll over on her belly? Of course, the exact age will vary by child but it was a helpful reference. Since this book covers mainly the first year, as new parents, we were less likely to get overwhelmed by the breadth of data.

The Baby Book, Sears, Little Brown and Company, 2003

Dr. Sears and his clan seem to know everything there is to know about child rearing. His book is an encyclopedia of information on behavioral and medical issues. For example, when Sidney was teething she was cranky and drooled a lot. Or more like Sidney was cranky and drooling a lot and *The Baby Book* enabled us to identify the symptoms as teething and suggest some ways to soothe her.

Caring for Your Baby and Young Child, Birth to Age 5, American Academy of Pediatrics, Steven P. Shelov, editor in chief, Bantam, 2009

In some ways this covers the same ground as *What to Expect in the First Year*. However, there is a not so subtle milestone at age one where babies stop being infants. So having a book that goes beyond that is very helpful. For example, our doctor insisted our kids could not drink whole milk until they were twelve months old. Babies less than twelve months old <u>must</u> have their car seats facing the rear and it's not until they turn one that you can face them front. You might say childhood really starts after the first year. This book was a wealth of knowledge that extended past the first 12 months because in the next year they start to crawl, and walk, and talk and it was great to have some perspective on that.

Let's be clear. No book is a substitute for a good pediatrician. And since the science behind child rearing is constantly evolving, these books get updated on a regular basis. We found them to be an excellent and comforting reference.

Chapter Three - Courses to Take

Getting ready for and researching the birth of your first child should go a lot further that reading a few books. There are a plethora of courses you can take. We stuck to what we considered the basics: birthing, infant care, and a hospital tour. Not surprisingly, the birthing course gave us an understanding of how best to help my wife through the birth, while the two infant care courses taught us invaluable lessons about regular and emergency care.

Birthing Classes

Before you can choose a birthing class, you have to choose your preferred method of birth. There are two basic choices: cesarean (AKA, c-section) and natural. There's oodles of research for each, and I won't go into pros and cons, because in the end it's usually a personal choice. Our choice was natural childbirth as we didn't want to take unnecessary risks with surgery, and have unneeded scars, and we felt that scheduling a birth, as people do with c-sections, took away some of the magic of giving birth. That said, there are some very good reasons why people have c-sections.

Most hospitals offer a "birthing" class of some sort. We found that many of these pushed a more medical approach with the use of epidurals. Since we wanted a more natural approach, Sandy researched the different birthing methods and found one that fit our personal needs, style, feelings: the Bradley method of natural childbirth or "husband-coached childbirth." There is also the Lamaze method that stresses breathing and HypnoBirthing, which you may infer from the name, involves self-hypnosis and relaxation. The Bradley course that we attended together was a 12 weeks and stressed relaxation. In addition to being very helpful and informative, it really kept us close, and it helped prepare me for the delivery room. I thought I'd be sick, or faint, but I was great. Ask Sandy. There's more about this in **Going to, and in, the Hospital**. Just remember to be flexible because things don't always go as planned. For us, each delivery was very different and not much went as planned. By the way, no matter how tired, how sore, how much you want to sit down, nothing you're going through is as hard as what your wife is going through. Suck it up. Don't complain. If you do, you'll hear about it for the rest of your life. Not to mention you'll be insensitive.

Newborn Care Classes

We affectionately referred to this basic infant care course as the "how not to kill your baby" course. It was given at a local hospital. It is an inherent trait for us men to think, and feel, we can do it all ourselves, fix anything and not ask for directions. For me, having and caring for a baby was no different. I figured I could do it all myself and/or figure it out as I went along. That may have been true. However, it was nice to hear from an experienced nurse/mom what to expect in the first days. The classes cover things like giving a bath, cleaning the stub of the umbilical cord (yeah, that's right, it's still there when you go home), changing a diaper, nursing, bottle feeding, swaddling, bonding, what to do when you drop the baby (just kidding).

Note: See **Everyday Living** for more information of nursing, bottle feeding and burping, *Gas Relief via Swaddling* in the **Lessons** section for the ins and outs of swaddling, and **Keeping Clean** for the low-down on cleaning the umbilical cord and bathing.

Infant CPR

The closer you get to the delivery date of your first child, the less you want to give up your Saturdays. They really are the last free weekends you'll have for a long time. However, infant CPR is a must. I was a senior lifesaver and took CPR classes in high school. That was a long time ago. Things change. Not just that, but infant CPR is different than adult CPR. It was time well spent. We felt confident about giving care in an emergency. I found out (after the fact) that my wife put what she learned to good use. When we were at a family gathering and Sidney, 13 months old, got her hands on a cashew nut. She didn't know how to chew it and started to choke. Sandy swiftly and confidently put Sidney over her arm, firmly whacked her back and dislodged the nut. I shudder to think what would have happened had we not given up four hours of a Saturday afternoon. Well worth it.

Hospital Tour

Choosing which hospital to use for the delivery of your child is a balance between convenience and knowing where your doctor or midwife has attending rights. Once you've decided on a hospital, I recommend a brief tour. It will take another afternoon of your life, but it's time well spent. It will give you an understanding of the layout. Where's the food? Something every guy needs to know. If you're there in the middle of the night you'll need to be able to find the vending machines. Where is the cafeteria? Where do I park? What entry do we come in? All this and more for less time than it took Gilligan to get shipwrecked.

Chapter Four - Going to, and at, the Hospital

The old cliché, "Is your bag packed?" is no joke. Sometimes you just get no warning. Babies have been known to come as many as eight weeks early. So planning ahead is your best ally. They will teach you in birthing classes that as labor progresses contractions slowly get closer together going from ten minutes down to about two minute apart over the space of several hours. This gives you time to plan, get to the hospital, call people, etc. Don't count on things going as planned. Sandy's labor with Sidney, our first, progressed so quickly that we went from easy ten-minute intervals to heavy two-minute intervals inside of forty minutes. Granted, what we went through with Sidney was quick, but good planning not only got us there in one piece, but it also helped things run smoothly once we were arrived. Planning not only includes packing, but also making sure you have an infant seat properly installed in your car.

You're there for support, so make sure you listen to your wife. While getting your wife safely to the delivery room is your primary concern, she knows her body, so it's her call about what she needs. Unless she's in real danger, do what she says. When we got to the hospital Sandy insisted on walking from the parking lot to the hospital entrance but had to stop literally every minute to lie across a pile of pillows to deal with her contractions. I wanted to put her in a wheelchair in spite of her complaints. But, to this day, she insists this would not only have ruined the experience for her and made her really mad, it also would have been exceptionally uncomfortable. In the hospital one of the attendants insisted Sandy get in a wheelchair. If I had it to do over, I would have stopped this, as it caused her considerable pain. There were just a few expletives in the elevator on the way up to the maternity ward.

Who's Watching the Kids?

With your first pregnancy if all goes as planned, when your wife goes into labor, you simply jump in the car and head over to the hospital. No advanced planning necessary, except of course to make sure you're packed. With subsequent kids it's not so simple. I recommend you have battle plans for child care that cover multiple situations. That may seem like overkill, but the issues are completely different if your wife goes into labor at 2 AM as opposed to 2 PM. If labor progresses quickly, as it did with Sidney, it's a completely different story than the slow, overnight stay we had ahead of the birth of our second child, Ellie. So you'll need contingencies for these different scenarios. For example, if your family is coming from out of town, you need someone who can get to the house quickly and watch the kid(s). He or she may only need to stay until your family arrives, but if your family wants to be at the hospital, you need to be ready for that too. The world stops when your wife goes into labor and if you don't have things arranged in advance, it can get tricky.

<u>What to Pack</u>

For you:

Plan on being awake, and tired, for a long time. You may be in the hospital for two to four nights. I went through five years of Architecture school with almost no sleep and I can't remember ever being as tired as I was when Sidney was born. At the hospital you'll get to sleep in an incredibly uncomfortable reclining chair. Or, if you're really lucky, an equally uncomfortable pull-out couch. You'll want comfortable clothes for yourself. Here's what I suggest:

- ☐ Comfortable pants for sleeping
- ☐ Underwear
- ☐ Socks
- ☐ Slippers
- ☐ Jeans
- ☐ Comfy shirt
- ☐ Shaving kit including:
  - o Brush or comb
  - o Toothbrush
  - o Toothpaste
  - o Deodorant
  - o Razor (and shaving cream)

For her:

She'll change out of her clothes and into hospital stuff when you get there. However, after the birth, when she's cleaned up, she'll want comfortable bedclothes and may feel better in her own clothes as opposed to hospital-wear. And no matter what she says she wants to wear, tell her she must pack some maternity clothes. She simply won't shrink to her pre-pregnancy size overnight and "normal" clothes will be very uncomfortable. Giving birth can get pretty funky, so she will probably want a shower after the first night (assuming the doctor allows it). Make sure shampoo and makeup go in the overnight bag. Here's what I suggest:

- ☐ Nice bathrobe for receiving guests
- ☐ Socks
- ☐ Slippers
- ☐ Comfy maternity pants
- ☐ Comfy shirts
- ☐ Makeup kit including shampoo and a hair dryer

For the baby:

You may want to have a nice change of clothes to bring your baby home in. We dressed Sidney and Ellie in the same outfit that Sandy came home in as a baby. The hospital will probably provide diapers, wipes and long-sleeve T-shirts. You should bring:

- ☐ Receiving blanket or two (see **Clothing, Stuff to Wear** for more information)
- ☐ Hat
- ☐ Some seasonally appropriate outerwear
- ☐ Diaper bag with diapers, wipes, onesies and bottles if you're not planning on breast feeding
- ☐ **Don't forget your properly installed car seat**

Other stuff to bring:

There is the off chance the labor will be slow and boring, as it was for us with Ellie and Calvin. We brought books, magazines and movies. In the end, we sat up all night talking about being parents, our kids, life together, and how much we love each other and didn't need all the stuff we brought with us, but you never know.

Money for the cafeteria and plenty of quarters for the vending machines are a must. With all due respect to the caterers who run the kitchens in the hospital, there is still a stigma that the food is horrible. And while that might not always be the case, if you're up at three in the morning, the cafeteria won't be open, hence the quarters. A bottle of water and a Snickers bar can go a long way in the middle of the night.

This may sound a little gross, but your wife's "bottom" is going to be very sore and swollen. Our hospital was very stingy with good ice-packs, so they'd stuff ice in rubber gloves. Before you pack get some good sports ice packs, the kind you squeeze to activate. She'll really appreciate having them. In list form, that's:

- ☐ Books and/or magazines
- ☐ Movies and something to play them on
- ☐ Music and something to play it on
- ☐ Quarters for the vending machine
- ☐ Ice packs
- ☐ Bottled water
- ☐ Snickers bars or some other handy treat/energy food
- ☐ Extra pillows

Put all this into an overnight duffel you can throw over your shoulder so you'll have a free hand to help your wife get from the car to the delivery room.

A Note about Nurses

There's one person who got very little press when researching and discussing our time in the hospital. A person who was incredibly important to the birth of our children and who gave us peace of mind, expert advice and gentle care. I'm speaking abut the labor and delivery nurse. I don't believe you have anything to say about how the delivery nurse gets assigned to you, but all of those we interacted with were fantastic. Your doctor or midwife may be in and out of the room throughout the laboring process. That leaves the care of the mother during much of the labor to the delivery nurse. LISTEN to her. She knows how things work and the tricks of laboring. When we had an issue with one of the practices we were working with, it was the delivery nurse who was able to give me some off-the-record advice and help us make a decision about which practice was better for us.

In the Delivery Room

All right, crunch time. You've had your fun (nine months ago), you've done your research, you've made your choices about doctors and midwifes. Now you're in the delivery room. In our hospital we labored and delivered in the same room, which looked like any typical hospital room. There was a side table and a little cabinet for clothing. Your doctor, or midwife, will be present along with the labor and delivery nurse.

You also have to decide who else will be in the delivery room. On some of the videos we saw in birthing class the whole family was there. That wasn't for us. I was the only one there for Sandy when Sidney was born. With Ellie and Calvin, we invited Sandy's mom. It wasn't as weird as I thought it would be and having an extra set of hands really helped. She was able to slip Sandy some ice chips, help rub her back or just be another supportive presence. I really liked the intimacy of being there for Sandy.

Delivery Time

Sandy's labor progressed very rapidly with our first child. She was on her knees on the bed intensely laboring one minute and the next minute the nurse and midwife were turning her onto her back and getting Sandy's feet into the stirrups. The midwife, who had been sitting at the table filling out some paperwork, stopped her pen mid-sentence, looked up and asked, "Did I just hear a push?" Believe it or not, there's a different sound made from pushing than from laboring (and by saying "laboring," I in no way want to belittle what she was going through). It was kind of comical, one minute our midwife was in street clothes, the next she's in full medical gear including a gown, surgical pants, gloves and, I kid you not, a full face mask. She laughed and told us you never know how fast things will come out. Now, all that said, the next two deliveries were completely different, though the delivery room and the full battle gear for delivery were the same. I think it's safe to say that the biggest difference between the first baby and the others was that with the others we knew what to expect.

We brought a music player to play soothing songs and/or sounds during delivery. Since we thought we might be laboring for a long time, we brought Snickers bars for me to snack on. Women in labor generally don't want to eat and in some cases are not allowed to if they are going under anesthesia. Some hospitals can be stingy with pillows so the extra pillows we brought came in handy. Having the pillows was dumb luck. We actually brought them for me to use at night when I got to sleep in that incredibly (un)comfortable hospital chair/bed.

Pain Medication (for Your Wife)

Natural childbirth has a couple of flavors: good old waiting around for it to happen or induced. On top of that, each of these can be either with or without pain meds. For us, "natural" childbirth involved no drugs at all, but you have to decide what's best for you. Your wife may get to a point she can't take the pain any longer, or she may not want to face the pain at all. The two of you have to decide, in advance, how you want to deal with that, but it's okay to change your mind later. One thing we learned is that the hospital staff will have your best interests in mind and when they see your wife in pain they may suggest some pain medication. If your wife doesn't want any medication you need to be clear up front with the staff that you don't want them to make the suggestion. She'll ask, more like demand, medication if she needs it. Sandy had no pain drugs whatsoever for any of our children. At the other end of the spectrum was our sister-in-law who ran to the hospital for an epidural at the very first contraction. There's no right or wrong to this. Your job is to be supportive and care for your wife. According to Sandy, all of the women on our birthing class intended to go drug free, but many of them ended up getting some type of medication.

How You Fit in during Delivery

Do whatever she needs. Her mouth will probably get really dry from heavy breathing and mild/severe panic. Fortunately the hospital will have plenty of ice chips. Occasionally slipping one into her mouth may be helpful. Sandy had heavy back labor with Sidney and needed hard back rubbing during each contraction. Unlike "regular" labor where the pain is concentrated in the abdomen, back labor pain is concentrated in the lower back and Sandy felt like Sidney was trying to come out through her lower back. We brought a wooden massage tool from the Body Shop for such an occasion, and during Sandy's labor I was pushing on it so hard I thought I was going to push it through her back. No matter what, no matter how exhausted you get, never, ever, say you're tired. And don't, under any circumstances, take offense to anything she says. Women all react differently to the pain they're in. Some can be touched, rubbed and comforted. Some don't want you to touch them and hate you for "doing this to them."

As a man, your natural reaction to all this may be to try and fix it. Guess what? You can't. In the delivery room you're somewhat powerless. Your job is to watch and help and do what you're told. What overcame that for me was the power of the situation. I stayed busy taking care of my wife and that's what it's really all about. I was also a little concerned about how things would look and smell. I thought I'd be totally grossed out when the baby's head started to come out. So much so that, at first, I was afraid to look. After all, what guy wants to spoil the mystery of what goes on "down there"? I've heard stories that vary from watching all the details of your wife's c-section to "there's no way I'm going to look." But I did look, and it was, well, different. There were quite a bit of fluids and a very briny smell. For all the things in my life that I've faced, watching my children, literally, come into the world is one of the most memorable. It was unlike than anything I've ever been through. But I didn't pass out. And there's still plenty of mystery.

How Mom Will Feel after Giving Birth

Giving birth is messy. Whatever you are wearing is going to get dirty. After the birth, when she's cleaned up, your wife may want comfortable bedclothes of her own. Remember, you're away from home, having just gone through one of the most tiring and intimate experiences of your life. She'll be sore and may need help getting to the bathroom, but she will want privacy when she gets there. When she goes to the bathroom the first time, it may be extremely painful. (A nurse will accompany her for this.) What shocked us most about this was that through all the research, all the classes, and all the training, this never came up. Granted, it's not something to look forward to, but know it's coming. She may be a little embarrassed that she needs your help and will want the comfort of your touch, but she will also need some time to herself. She may bleed a lot. (The hospital will provide ice and pads.).You'll also have a baby to care for. Do everything you possibly can to help you wife. She's more tired than you are!

What Happens to Baby Right after Delivery

Right after your baby is born Mom gets to hold her. They put matching ID tags on Baby and Mom, and we were told we couldn't leave the hospital unless they both matched. Then they take your baby away. In our case, that was to the other side of the birthing room. In some hospitals, it's to the nursery. This will be clarified on the hospital tour. They do a whole lot of stuff to baby that no one ever told us about, even on the tour. I just wanted to hold her. But first they have to weigh her, and take her vitals, and give her a bath, and wash her hair, and then she's cold so they have to put her under a heat lamp, which to me looked more like klieg lights, until she was warm. The bath was the most painful to watch. All three of our kids seemed cold and were crying. Because it's so routine to the nurses, they came off as unfeeling, but we're told this was all perfectly normal and harmless. It didn't feel that way. It took about an hour for each of our children to warm up enough that we could hold them. There is also stuff they have to do to "finish" with Mom and make sure she's okay and not bleeding. All this takes between one and two hours if there are no complications.

At some point they'll wheel your baby away to take the compulsory baby picture. You get to pick the hat from a wide variety of very ugly choices. I accompanied all our kids to "supervise" the photo-shoot. I'm sure there was nothing to worry about with regard to safety or our baby getting mixed up with someone else's, but being new (overprotective) parents we didn't want our babies out of our sight, not even for a minute, even with the matching ID tags. The hospital also may give you the choice of sending your baby to the nursery so Mom can sleep. The nursery is a room with rows of tiny baby-filled cribs. It generally is overlooked through a glass wall from the corridor. The corridor where, in a movie, the actors stand looking in at the babies and dole out clichés. It's your choice whether you want to accompany baby for the picture or send her off to the nursery so you guys can sleep. Make sure to check with your hospital on your choices and their policies regarding the nursery.

Expect visitors. Family will undoubtedly come through sometime after the birth. The people who were waiting all that time will be anxious to see Mom and Baby. Depending on the time of day or night and how tired Mom is, it's your job to move them along. For us, a lot more people came through on the second day. It seemed like everyone I hadn't seen in twenty years wanted to get a look at my offspring. If your wife is too tired to deal with it, you need to shoo them away.

The First Day with Your Newborn

Here's where all the training from all those classes you took kicks in. You get to change a diaper on a real baby. (Yippee!!!) I never babysat as a youngster nor do I have any younger siblings and was completely grossed out by the thought of changing my nephew's diaper. You know what? It truly is different when it's your own. But nothing prepares you for the first poop. It's this dark brown tar-ish stuff called merconium. It may seem gross but it's perfectly natural, and practically odor free. It's just a little sticky. They'll give you a chart in the hospital to count liquid and solid output for the first five days or so. It's important to know that what's going into your baby is coming out. Although, if you're breast feeding, it's hard to know how much is going in, so you have to pay close attention to "output."

Don't expect to get a good night's sleep. The first night, the nurse will come in to check Mom and Baby's "vitals" every hour or so. It's nice to know you're getting good care, but it can be very tiresome. If Mom and Baby are healthy you can probably set down some rules for the second night, such as don't wake us up until morning rounds, so you can get some sleep. But it doesn't mean they'll listen. In our hospital the night crew would come in banging around when it suited them seemingly without a care in the world about waking Mom and Baby. From their point of view, they had to get in rounds before the shift change, but it was somewhat frustrating.

Oh yeah, and Dad, when the baby cries, you get up, change her, and give her to Mom to nurse. Or, if you decided to skip breast feeding and go straight to formula, feed her yourself and let Mom sleep. Yes, get your tired butt out of bed or that extremely uncomfortable chair you're sleeping in and help out. Remember, Mom is way more tired than you.

Staying in the Hospital

Most medical plans dictate how long you are covered to stay in the hospital. Ours was two days for natural birth, four for cesarean. Stay as long as you possibly can. Yes, you're not in the comfort of your own home, but you're also getting excellent care and you don't have to do any dishes. Plus, your baby will get to see the pediatrician multiple times and you'll have lots of questions. It is harder to stay both nights with the subsequent babies because you'll have a little one at home. We were fortunate that Grandma came to stay and took care of the kids for our second and third. It was wonderful watching the "older" kids meet the baby for the first time.

I spent both nights with Sandy when all three kids were born. You will feel much better after the first night if you shower, shave and change your clothes, although you'll still probably be totally exhausted. To the hospital, you (the dad) don't exist, meaning the hospital will bring meals for your wife and you get to schlep around the hospital in your dingy clothes and slippers to the cafeteria to get something to eat. Ask the nurses for take-out menus from local restaurants. They usually have them at the nurse's station. The second night after Sidney was born we had dinner brought in from our favorite restaurant and avoided hospital food altogether.

Updating the Family

We had people in the waiting room for all three deliveries, but it never occurred to us how they were feeling. We stayed completely focused on Sandy and the baby and they were dying to know how Mom and Baby were doing; not to mention whether it was a boy or a girl, since we chose not to find out the gender in the ultrasounds. They can wait. However, you do need to prepare the family so they understand that it takes about two hours *after* the baby is born to get everything set and be ready for visitors. There are also ways you can update them like sending a nurse, or if there's more than one person helping Mom, then one of you can go or you can just tell them to get over it. It's totally up to you.

Chapter Five - Other Tidbits

There are a few odd tidbits that don't fit easily into the previous chapters but a definitely part of preparing for a baby. There are important decisions to make about pediatric care, whether and where to store the cord blood and what to expect when you first arrive home. Lastly, I've included some insight into how to announce to the world that you have passed the torch, created an heir, had a baby.

Cord Blood Storage

With the rapidly expanding field of cord blood and stem cell research, it is highly likely that if you or your child ever get a life-threatening disease, like diabetes or leukemia, through the use of your child's cord blood he or she may be completely cured. So we think that saving our children's cord blood made a lot of sense. This can only help your family. Although prices may change, at press time the initial processing fee was about $2,000 and then it's about $100 per year for frozen storage for the facility we chose. Think of it as another form of insurance.

This technology has come a long way since my nephew was born in 1999. Sandy (research junkie [read expert]) researched the top five storage sites and we chose Cord Blood Research (CBR), which is associated with the University of Arizona. Although they cost a little more than some other facilities, if the company ever goes out of business the university will guarantee the storage of our cord blood forever.

Life at Home

So, you've got this baby and you're ready to go home. With our first baby, neither one of us had left the hospital for two days. The light of day was jarring, yet welcome. You can't leave the hospital with your baby without a properly installed infant seat. But before I get into the baby products you'll need, let me make a few additional points about home life. First, it will be different from anything you've ever experienced before. You have time for only one thing: taking care of baby. It's new, it's different, it's exhausting, and it's the most amazing and fun thing you'll ever do. But in the beginning you're clueless, so here are a few pointers to help you along.

Family Help

Like most men I want to do it all myself. The thought of having my mother-in-law around for two weeks was, at first, disconcerting. Don't get me wrong, I love my mother-in-law. It's just that I don't like to admit it when I need help. Here's the kind of help we needed, and got. Someone to take care of **us** so we could take care of Sidney; someone who would sit up with Sidney at night when she was having trouble adjusting to life outside the womb. Someone to gently point out that maybe we should change her diaper first, and then nurse her. Because when we did the reverse, she fell asleep nursing and then we woke her up again changing her diaper. The list goes on: she'd do the grocery shopping, the cooking and cleaning, answer the phone, **let us nap.** She was also an excellent teacher. That experience thing goes a long way. She raised three kids, after all. There's a flip side to all this, though. If your "helper" isn't helping and is driving you both up a wall, especially if she's driving your wife up a wall, it's your job to give that person the boot. Remember, this isn't about you. It's about Mom and Baby. So if you're uncomfortable and your wife is loving life, you'll have to get over it.

Visitors

The message here is the same whether someone is staying the night or just dropping by. He or she takes care of you, not the other way around. This was a mantra in every book I read. Limit the number of guests that stop by. Set limits on visiting hours. Anyone who comes by expecting to be entertained isn't welcome. <u>Oh yeah, and everyone washes their hands before picking up the baby; it's a germ thing</u>. I can't stress the importance of hygiene. Many people don't realize just how sensitive newborns are to germs and every outsider carries them. If your baby gets a fever of more than 102 during the first two months of life, she may need to be hospitalized.

Finding a Pediatrician

We spent hours, actually days, researching pediatricians. You *must* interview them. Bring a list of questions. Look at websites like www.ivillage.com or www.parentingsquad.com for a list of questions to ask your pediatrician. You can also look at www.babycenter.com for questions and pointers about finding a pediatrician. If a prospective doctor won't grant an interview, don't use him or her. Check references. Everyone you speak to should absolutely love their pediatrician. Think about it, would you want your child seen by someone with a reference of "eh"?

Let me stress the importance of personal referrals because we did all this. Found a guy we loved. His references were fantastic. Then we went to our first visit and got one of the partners who had the personality of paste. His reaction to our list of questions was "All new parents ask that...blah, blah, blah." Well we had never asked these questions and wanted a little more enthusiasm from our child's doctor. We were fortunate that our midwife had a pediatrician she adored. Exactly the kind of recommendation you want. We quickly changed practices and never looked back. So ask around. There are some great doctors out there. Just make sure they love working with kids in addition to being "qualified."

Birth Announcements

Many people send out birth announcements, which come in a variety of shapes and sizes. Some are simple postcards, others get stuffed in envelopes. You can order them online or make them yourself. I would opt for the former, as you will most likely be exhausted. Either way, you're going to need a good picture of your baby. "Good" does not mean it has to be professionally taken, but that is certainly an alternative. We were very happy with the quality and service we got from www.storkavenue.com. However, there are dozens of services you can find online including www.shutterfly.com and www.flikr.com. Most will have do-it-yourself layouts and offer a variety of addressing and mailing services. For more information on when to take pictures see *Take the Pictures Early, Your Baby Will Get Acne* in **Section 3 – Stuff About Living.**

Section 2 - The Stuff

There is a plethora of stuff that you need to care for, clean, transport and play with a baby. If you decide to go with one manufacturer, you can pretty much get everything to color coordinate. We gave it a shot, but never got there. Some items were out of stock, or the pattern was discontinued. For others, we just liked a different manufacturer or the "best" was made by someone else. Looking back, I'd say it wasn't that important for the basic stuff. It's never, let me be clear, **NEVER**, all in the same place at the same time, except, maybe, at the baby shower.

We spent a considerable amount of time picking furniture and designing the nursery. This was as much for the baby as it was for us so we would feel comfortable in the room. We spent a lot of late nights in there. We planned ahead, but in some ways we planned too far ahead. For example, we intended the nursery to be used for all our children, but that turned out to be wishful thinking. After we put an addition on our house and moved our bedroom upstairs, we were no longer comfortable having our children downstairs. You cannot predict how parenthood will change your perceptions about safety.

I have broken the "stuff" down into categories that correspond roughly to how you'll use it. In each section there is an overview of the product, along with some notes on what we learned, liked or disliked.

Chapter Six - Car Seats

It's a bit of a cliché to say that car seats come in all shapes and sizes, but there is a variety that you should be aware of. They each serve its purpose and can generally be delineated by height, weight and age. (Also see the **Stuff for Traveling** for information on keeping them clean whilst flying.)

The "Latch System"

Before I get into the actual seats, a quick word on attaching them to your car. If your car is a model year 2003 or after, it has the "latch system." Although the latch system became standard on all new cars put on the road after 2003, it was included on some made as early as 2001. Check in your owner's manual to be sure. A latch-equipped car will have metal catches about ¼" thick welded to the car frame in the space between the seat and seat back where the seatbelt sticks out and/or disappears. The catches look like a karabiner cut in half length-wise. Latch-equipped car seats have special clasps that attach to these catches. It is a far easier and superior method of attaching the seat, or base, to the car. An infant or toddler seat attached properly with the latch system, coupled with the appropriate tether at the top, becomes virtually a part of your car.

Seating Requirements

Where your baby, or child, can sit and what direction he or she is allowed to face vary by state. The differences can be maddening. In our state, before age one our babies **had** to face rear, plus there was a weight restriction. Once our babies weighed 20 pounds *and* were one year old they could face forward. Since we live very close to a state border we needed to make sure we were in compliance anytime we crossed state lines. Even more complex was a trip to Grandma's where we went through four states. The best place to bone up on the latest standards is the National Highway Traffic Safety Administration (NHTSA) website. It's got charts and links and pictures (no lions and tigers and bears), oh my. Check it out at http://www.nhtsa.gov/Safety/CPS.

Infant Seat

Call it what you like, infant seat, baby seat, car seat, but your baby may not leave the hospital with without it. Like all things baby, infant seats have height and weight limits. For example, the seats we had were good up to 18 pounds or twenty-six inches which ever came first. Since you'll be carting your newborn around in one of these for several months, you may want to choose one that comes with a separate base. You attach the base into the car, and the seat snaps into it. Make sure the base is adjustable because the seat must be within a certain angle for prime safety. The combination of infant seat angle and the angle of the seat in your car will vary, hence the need for adjustability. The reason for the separate base is so you can remove the seat with a <u>sleeping</u> baby in it and bring it inside without waking Baby. You can also buy an additional base if you have a second car so you don't have to foot the bill for an entire additional car seat.

In our infant care classes the trainers told us they were amazed at how many people didn't put the seats in correctly. You have to read the owner's manual from your car *and* the instructions from the seat. Therefore, it's a good idea to take your car with the seat installed to the local police or fire station after you've installed it so they can verify it's in safely. Yes, this goes against the manly, "I can do it myself," but get over it, these guys are pros. If you are attaching the car seat or base with a seatbelt, there is a special clasp that comes with the seat you may need to use depending on the seatbelt design. It's a pain, but remember whose life it is anyway.

You should never put your baby in an infant seat with a heavy winter coat on because it reduces the effect of the straps. If you have your baby in the winter, there are cozies you can get that completely cover the top of the seat and zip up to cover your baby. This lets you keep him warm without a coat. Remember, the car seat will already be warm because it will be inside the house with you.

Toddler Seat

Toddler seats look a lot like mini wing chairs you attach to your car. They generally have five-point harnesses and are the next step after infant seats. Since all our kids grew out of their infant seats before their first birthday we needed a "convertible" toddler seat, meaning one that can face rear or front. One of the things that makes a regular toddler seat "convertible" is that the base has an angle adjustment so the pitch can be changed when you turn it around. They come with the same attachment flavors as infant seats: seat belt or the latch system.

Booster Seat

The last type of special seat you'll need is a booster seat, which are kind of like a safer version of sitting on a phone book. Their purpose to raise your child's shoulders to the right height so the seat belt comes across it in the right place. Many booster seats resemble a small, legless dining room armchair with a padded seat. Some have arms that adjust in height. The first seat we got also had a back that resembled a mini wing chair. This gave them a place for their little heads to rest when they fell asleep in the car. We eventually outgrew the backs and they ended up stacked in the basement like wood waiting for a bonfire. One of the nicest things about booster seats is that they are very inexpensive. We ended up with so many that we could fill both cars with our kids and their friends.

The requirements for the changeover from a toddler seat to a booster are not as strict, at least in our state. This may vary by state, so reference the NHTSA site to be sure. We wanted to keep our kids in the five-point restraint for as long as possible, so it was our personal choice to keep them in the toddler seat until they were four. I have to admit, getting them into a booster is far easier than a five-point, so we were all too happy to let go of the toddler seats when Calvin turned four.

Car Setup – Multiple Cars
When we first had the kids, we had no garage and parked in tandem in the driveway, so we didn't want to worry about which car was in back. Therefore, when we had Sidney, we

wanted the flexibility of being able to travel with either car. This was relatively easy with an infant seat because all it required was the purchase of a second base. Once she was out of the infant seat, the cost to obtain the same flexibility went up significantly because what I consider to be good toddler seats cost over $250 each. However, we were certain we'd be having another baby and figured we'd eventually need to use two toddler seats, so we set up both cars the same way. However, with three kids it wasn't so easy and, ultimately, we had to be more careful about parking and juggling cars.

It's amazing how your priorities change. When Sidney was born, I wouldn't have thought twice about getting more toddler seats. Two years later I was thinking about saving for college. Bottom line is, you have to decide what makes sense from a cost and convenience point of view based on your budget, your physical parking/driving arrangement, and how big you think your family will get.

Chapter Seven - Getting Around

Getting around with your baby may require a few accessories. Whether you're going somewhere in the car or not, you'll eventually want some way of transporting Baby when you're walking. There are a number of choices. Not only are there several different types of strollers, there are various slings, harnesses and backpacks too. Top that off with a diaper bag and you're ready for the day out with your little angel.

Strollers

We started out, as many new parents do, assuming we needed the biggest, best, most well-equipped stroller out there. To me, stroller always meant the big, clunky, single seat, basket underneath, folding canopy with a tray, four-wheel deal. We started with one of these after we tested a few. The one we landed on was part of an "all-in-one" system (see below for more information). The things that drove our choice were the quality and reputation of the car seat that came with such a system, and whether the stroller had a cup holder for the person pushing it. That's right; cup holder was at the top of the list: think coffee or bottled water. But make sure the holder is deep, because your bottle of water will tip out every time you hit a bump if it is too shallow. One day we met a woman while shopping who was pushing an umbrella stroller with pneumatic wheels. This is a bit unusual so I asked why she didn't use a bigger stroller. She said she'd been through them all and had about six strollers in her garage. In the end, this simple umbrella stroller was all she needed. I thought she was exaggerating. Funny thing is that when all was said and done, we ended up with about six strollers. Guess which one we used the most? You got it: the umbrella stroller.

One thing we realized after using the large stroller for a while was that, because of its size, it was cumbersome for Sandy to get it in and out of the trunk of the car. Depending on the size of your vehicle, it may also fill the entire trunk, which isn't good because you'll need all the space you can get for the other stuff you'll be hauling around.

Some other things we found important to have in or on a stroller:

- Wheels: the bigger and the softer, the better. They'll do a better job of absorbing the bumps, going over curbs, and keeping Baby asleep. In fact, some of the newer top-end strollers have pneumatic wheels. (A guy's particular heaven.)

- Basket: A basket underneath is a must (also the bigger, the better). You'll be amazed at how much stuff you're going to try to cram in there when you're shopping.

- Canopy: The more adjustable, the better. This really becomes evident when you are strolling into the late afternoon sun. If the canopy doesn't come down far enough, you end up draping a baby blanket from the canopy. Baby doesn't like the sun in her eyes and she'll let you know.

- Serving Tray: One with a cup holder is a must, although it's not available on most umbrella strollers. This may sound funny, but it was a place not only for cups, but also for food, toys and crayons as well. Our cup holder had Goldfish in it more often that a sippy cup.

All-in-One Systems

These systems include a stroller, car seat, and car seat base, and are intended to let you grow into the stroller. When your baby is first born, she can't sit up, so it's important to have a stroller that can accommodate this.

These do so by allowing you to attach the car seat to the stroller. Once she can sit up, you can place her in the stroller and leave the car seat in the car. The all-in-one system is a great time and money saver when shopping. However, if we had it to do over again, we would buy a separate car seat and base, stroller, and car seat stroller. (See *Car Seat Stroller* below.)

Car Seat Stroller

An affordable alternative to a massive full feature stroller is a car seat stroller. This is basically a frame that you set your infant seat into. It is inexpensive, lightweight, folds very compact, and is adjustable for just about any make/model of car seat. You can use it until your baby can sit up and can then jump right to an umbrella stroller if that suits you. Ellie grew so fast that we didn't need to get one, but we used one when we had Calvin and loved it. Why not with Sidney? No one told us about them.

Jogging Stroller

To state the obvious, a jogging stroller is for transporting your baby while you're out for a jog. However, the way they're built and the size of the wheels make them convenient for getting around on any rough terrain. They generally have more elaborate, five-point seat belts than regular strollers. We found the most important feature of jogging strollers is the size of the wheels. The larger the wheel, the better it is for running. For the baby, it's important to make sure the canopy is adjustable and can flip way down in front of him for the times you are running into the sun. From a practical standpoint, you'll want to choose one that is fairly light. I'm sure you can spend ridiculous money to get one that weighs less than an ounce, but unless you're planning to run competitively with your baby, it's probably not worth it. It is also important that there is a wrist strap and a hand break.

We made the mistake of looking for our jogging stroller in the same place we shopped for all our other baby goods. While the big box "baby store" had a decent selection, we subsequently found much nicer joggers in places that specialize in outdoor gear, like REI or Eastern Mountain Sports, and online at www.joggingstroller.com or www.babyjogger.com. We ultimately got, and were very happy with, one made by Bob (yep, Bob).

Umbrella Stroller

These get their name from the way they fold up and have hooked handles that make them look like an umbrella. They are very light, compact, and affordable. We chose to go with one that would recline and had a canopy, which cost us a little more. The only drawback we found was the lack of a tray or a cup holder (both hard to find in an umbrella stroller). Our umbrella stroller got, by far, more use than any of our other strollers. One other thing to keep in mind is that new-born babies can't sit up, so if your umbrella stroller doesn't recline, you'll have to wait until she's sitting up before you can use it.

Double Stroller

Paper or plastic? There is one basic, personal issue you have to resolve when shopping for a double stroller: whether the kids sit in tandem (front and back) or side-by-side. I'm sure they both have their merits. To be clear, double strollers are for transporting two children at the same time. There are also strollers made for transporting three kids at a time, but more than that and you're into custom-made stuff. We chose (read: guessed) side-by-side so the kids could interact. We weren't disappointed. No mystery on the features we wanted; see the list in *Strollers*. Our side-by-side stroller folded like a double-wide folding chair and then folded in thirds, making it very compact. It also had a shoulder strap, so it was easy to transport.

Sit and Stand Stroller

When we were pregnant with Ellie this presented itself as an alternative to a double stroller. It had a regular seat in the front, with a frame to hold a car seat. In the back it had a platform our toddler could stand on, or if she was tired, she could turn around and face us on a bench seat. It's a neat idea and Sidney loved it — in the store. After that, she never wanted to ride in it. It may be great for some families, but it sat on our front porch collecting dust for six months before becoming part of a massive Craigslist offering.

Umbrella for the Stroller

To keep the sun out of Baby's eyes, we went the additional step of getting a clip-on umbrella for the stroller. The best ones have a flexible neck that let you tilt them in virtually any direction. Ours got so much use that we bought them in twos and threes because the bendy necks eventually gave out with heavy usage.

<u>Harness – (i.e. Bjorn)</u>

Once your baby can hold his head up, you may want an alternative way to carry him. Your arms can get tired holding a baby all the time and a harness frees your hands for other things. There are several types that you can use to strap your baby on. Make sure that the harness is fully and easily adjustable, as you will undoubtedly be sharing with your wife. The straps should be soft and wide or they'll dig into your back. The carrying pouch should be soft but firm for Baby. Lastly, the harness should be easily adaptable for facing the baby in (toward you) and out. Our first child, Sidney, got very fussy in the harness, at first. Then we tried facing her out and she was fine. She just wanted to see the world. Oh yeah, make sure it's machine washable. We used a harness made by Baby Bjorn and loved it.

<u>Sling</u>

You know how when you break your arm, you put it in a sling? A baby sling is based on that concept, only it's larger and some have padded edges. It is adjustable in length and fits around your neck. When your baby is small, he can fit into it in a more or less lying position. The literature for ours showed people using them to hold their toddlers in a sitting position. We have seen the occasional person using one, but it was not for us. We got one and tried it with our first two babies, but they were not comfortable. Our kids wanted to see what was going on around them and, I think, they felt hot and confined in the sling.

Baby Backpack

We're a fairly active family. So when we went on vacation in Maine we got a backpack to carry Sidney. We did some serious hiking, and on some of the trails we really should not have been on carrying a baby, but I was in good shape and no one got hurt. Having an excellent baby backpack made a big difference. I suggest you go to an "outdoor" store like Eastern Mountain Sports or REI for the best selection. Look for the same things you would in a regular backpack: a padded waist belt, padded shoulder straps, lightweight frame. Make sure the sling (where your baby sits) is adjustable so you can continue to use it as your baby grows. The height of the shoulder straps in relation to the waist belt should also be easily adjustable, which is very important if people of different heights (like you and your wife) are going to carry the pack. Our pack sat on legs that opened up when it was taken off. This way it could free-stand for easy loading and unloading. It also came with a detachable canopy that was great when it started to drizzle, pockets for our water bottles, and a detachable mini-pack we used for blankets and diapers. One thing I didn't like was that I couldn't reach my water bottle when hiking. So I attached a water bottle holder to one of the shoulder straps with a karabiner. We attached a mirror on a string so I could look back at whoever I was carrying. You may also want to attach a play toy or two to the backpack to keep your child occupied. You might like the scenery on a hike, but that colorful snake thingy is much more interesting to your child. We used the "chain links" (found in the **Play Toys** section) for attaching the toys. Just be careful with the things you attach to the pack to make sure he can't wrap anything around his neck.

Diaper Bag

Diaper bags come in a wide variety of colors, patterns, and sizes. Contrary to what the name implies, they're for much more than just diapers. This was one case where basic black, or navy, worked well to keep me in touch with my masculine side. These bags get used, moved, and tossed quite a bit. In our family, that meant they lasted about a year, so you may not be stuck with the first one your get. They are generally for one excursion at a time, meaning you'll reload back at the house between outings. While this seems like a simple concept, I remember calling a friend of mine who has four kids and asking what you do when you travel because I couldn't figure out how to get everything for the trip in the bag. There's more about this in *Packing for Travel* in the **Stuff for Traveling** section.

At first you put everything in the world in your diaper bag. When your baby is little you actually need more stuff in the bag. A good one will have a thermal compartment for food/bottles, an outer pouch to make bottles and sippy cups easy to access, and at least two main sections. The large section is for spare diapers, clothes, receiving blankets and toys. The smaller section should have dividers or compartments for wipes, medicine, snacks, and other little items. Also, make sure to get one with a changing pad. We found that a removable pad was best. Our first bag had it attached. This meant we never lost it, but we felt it wasn't the most convenient. For example, there wasn't enough room on the changing stations in public bathrooms for the bag and the pad. Most have a sealable section for soiled diapers. I never used it because I always found a place to throw those bad boys away.

Once your baby gets older, about 12 to 18 months you don't have to carry as much stuff. She's eating table food; diaper changes are less frequent, as are clothing changes. For most of the second year of Sidney's life we traveled with a small diaper bag. This had one main compartment that held a few diapers, wipes, one change of clothes, and a toy. Plus it had a small outer pouch for snacks and any medicine we might need.

As an alternative to a traditional diaper bag, large or small, you may want to consider a day-pack. When we were hauling stuff around for three children, and didn't want to carry more than one bag, our day-pack fit the bill. It had three sections of varying sizes so we could easily carry clothes, diaper, wipes, and toys; that's right, toys. Toys are an important part of any meal out because they keep your child entertained, so you can actually eat. The pack also had pouches on the outside to hold water bottles or sippy cups.

Chapter Eight - Stuff for Traveling

Traveling with a baby is a unique experience. In addition to all the stuff you're used to taking for you and/or your partner, you have to also pack for Baby. This goes well beyond clothes and diapers. You'll need toys, entertainment, and maybe a highchair. Depending on where you're going, you may also need a travel crib.

Travel Crib

Commonly known as a Pack-n-Play these cribs break down to an amazingly small size. They have a system of interlocking, folding arms that appear to have no chance of unfolding to make a rigid form. However, once you snap the magic twist lock at the bottom into place, they mysteriously transform into a mini crib. They are a must when traveling with a baby. Many hotels will provide them for you, although the cleanliness factor freaked out my wife so she refused to use them. At the very least I recommend you bring your own sheets. Also, many family members you may visit simply may not have a crib. My dad, for example, was a little challenged when it came to preparing for grandkids. Sandy's mom, on the other hand, set up a complete nursery.

You may want to get a travel crib that comes with an insert to adjust the height of the "mattress." You can use the higher position for an infant so she's easier to get in and out. When your baby can pull herself up to standing, you simply store the insert away and use the lower position. Make sure the sides are vented, which will not only help to keep baby cool in the hot summer months, but also provide much-needed fresh air.

We decided to get one with all the bells and whistles. Ours came with a changing station that fit over half the top of the crib and a tent-cover-netting thing for use outdoors to keep the bugs away. We never used these items. They got put away and lost, so it was not money well spent. If your nursery is on the second floor, a travel crib can also come in handy for naps on the first floor (for the baby).

Car Seat Entertainment

You know how you feel on a long airplane flight when you get that bulkhead seat? You're too far forward to see the movie and there's nothing in front of you but the wall. Once your baby gets to be about four to six months old that's how he'll feel in his car seat. He'll be facing the back seat with nothing to do. There are a variety of "toys" you can get that attach to the seat back so he has something to look at. Car seat entertainers are colorful mats that hang by the head rest and strap to the seat to stay in place. Not only do they give your baby something to look at, but many of them are "activated" when your child kicks them. A baby who's entertained is less likely to fuss.

You may also want to consider having some baby toys in the car so he has something to touch and put in his mouth. To avoid it constantly ending up on the floor get some plastic links (see **Play Toys**) and attach them to his seatbelt. Just make sure there's not so much slack that he can get it around his neck.

Car Seat Cover for the Plane

If you're taking a flight and renting a car when you get there, most rental agencies will rent you a car seat (for a mint). We did that once and weren't thrilled with the quality of the seat. Plus, there's really no way to know if the seat has ever been in an accident or how old it is. Look at is this way, would you buy a car seat from a total stranger at a garage sale? So the next time we flew, we brought our car seat with us. But since the cargo bay on the plane is not exactly clean, we bought, and used, an inexpensive car seat cover. It was made of genuine plastic, big enough for the toddler seat, zipped shut, and had a shoulder strap. When we traveled, the airline did not count it as an extra bag, so there were no extra fees. I stress the "when," because airlines have been going goofy finding ways to hit you with extra fees. Many of them don't consider a car seat or a stroller as part of the luggage count, but that could change anytime and may vary by airline.

Portable Highchair

This is a plastic, folding, adjustable booster seat with a tray. Some attach to the table with a clamp. Others strap to a kitchen chair. The clamp-on kind scared me, but I had a friend who used one and loved it. Ours was the strap-on type that folded down smartly into a compact carrying case and the straps wound up into the seat. It could be used with or without the tray. It was extremely handy on vacations or when we were traveling to places without highchairs. When Sidney was two we used it as a booster to make her place at the table a "big girl chair" so she could eat with us. Just keep in mind that nothing will ever get as funky as your highchair and this is no exception. Sandy used to take a steamer to it every few months to get all the crud off it.

Packing for Travel

I generally travel light. Before we had kids, Sandy and I could go away for a four-day weekend with one carry-on suitcase. Once you start traveling with a baby you'll notice that you've got a little more to carry. You will need to at least double the amount of clothing you bring for yourself. With a baby, your shoulders will forever have spit up on them. With a toddler, sticky fingers will always be wiping something on your pants. Indeed, I am convinced the major hidden cost of children is in the extra dry cleaning. So, the one suitcase for the two of you days are over.

For the baby, you'll need to pack a bag with enough clothes to have two to three outfits for each day. Also include enough diapers and wipes to last the trip if you want to avoid running to the store for more. However, if you're going on a week-long vacation and plan on doing a grocery store run when you get there, it may be easier to pick up a package of diapers at that time rather than to bring them in your luggage. Bring travel-sized baby shampoo, baby washcloths and (maybe) baby towels, at least for the first year or so. If you're staying at a hotel, you may find that the towels and washcloths tend to be a little rough.

Children crave routine. Travel disrupts this. Anything you can bring along that helps Baby feel at home will make bedtime easier. So, bring her favorite toys. If she's less than six months, you can get by with a few rattles in the diaper bag. Older than that, you'll need puzzles, balls, drums (Sidney had a baby bongo), stuffed animals, the crib entertainer. And don't forget the books. If she has a favorite story, make sure you bring it. When we went away with Sidney the first time, we were relieved to arrive at 11:30pm and have her fast asleep. Unfortunately, she woke up before we got to our room and was very disoriented. Having her favorite book was a charm to get her back to sleep. I'd hate to think what it would have been like without it.

The short list (this will vary by age):

- ☐ Your clothes
- ☐ Baby clothes
- ☐ Baby toys
- ☐ Travel crib
- ☐ Gymini (see **Stuff for Playing**)
- ☐ Bouncy seat
- ☐ Breast pump (if you're breast feeding)

- ☐ Diaper bag

- ☐ Stroller

- ☐ Extra diapers

- ☐ Portable highchair

- ☐ Bjorn harness

- ☐ Washcloths and towels

- ☐ Bottles

- ☐ Pacifiers (affectionately know as "puckies")

- ☐ Burp cloths (we used cloth diapers for this, see **Stuff for Keeping Clean**)

- ☐ Fingernail clippers

- ☐ Diaper cream

- ☐ Maybe most important: Medicine (see the **Medicine** section of **Safety and First Aid** for more on this.) Kids have way of getting sick when you're on the road, so having your staples handy will help them feel better and allow you all to get some rest.

This doesn't include the stuff you need for special trips, like presents for the holidays or the backpack if you're hiking. Oh yeah, and leave room for the dog.

Chapter Nine - Furniture

A typical nursery will have a crib and changing table, but also may have a glider (chair), wardrobe, end table, reading lamp and other comforts. It depends on how you intend to use the room, but chances are you'll be spending a lot of time there. When we were shopping for furniture for the nursery we ended up in a high-end, boutique baby furniture store. At the time we thought the salesman was very nice, knowledgeable and full of good advice. Of course, all salesmen want you to think that. We got some very nice furniture but may have done just as well shopping at Babies-R-Us or any other "big box" store. There are many places you can visit and research different brands of household furniture. However, for the baby furniture there aren't as many places to shop. I recommend furniture made out of solid wood, not veneer, with quality drawer tracks. Solid wood will better withstand the beating it's going to take in the nursery.

It is very important to allow enough time for delivery. Made-to-order furniture can take twelve weeks to arrive. Our glider (that's a chair, see below) was delayed a further three weeks. Big box stores may have more things in stock, so there's less of a wait. We made our purchase sixteen weeks in advance, and it barely made it to the house on time. At the end of the pregnancy you've got enough going on that you don't want to be worrying about your nursery furniture.

Crib

It's important that you understand the current safety standards for cribs, especially if you want to purchase one used. In 2011 the Consumer Product Safety Commission updated its standards for cribs. This included some changes to the standards for, but not the elimination of, drop-side cribs. Search its site http://www.cpsc.gov/onsafety for "crib" and you'll be brought to the latest data. You can also look in places like *Parenting* and *Consumer Reports*.

A lot about cribs is personal taste, as there are many possibilities when it comes to design. On some cribs the front can be removed, making it a toddler bed. We figured we'd have another baby in it before we'd need a "big girl bed," so we planned on making that purchase later.

One of the features we felt was important in a crib was the ease of raising and lowering the front panel. Did I mention there's a lot of guesswork as to how you will and won't use things? We never lowered the front panel to get our daughter out. Bear in mind that I'm six foot four and Sandy is five foot eleven, so lifting a baby over the rail was not as much of an issue for us. For my five-foot tall step-mother, it was a different story. However, the imagined importance of this feature was very different than our reality.

Two other things that we found very helpful: the ease of adjusting the mattress height and the drawer under the crib. When you first put your baby in the crib, he basically can't move. Eventually he will start to roll over. But until this point it's nice to have him up high so he's easier to get in and out, rub his belly and coo at. Once he starts to sit up, you lower the mattress, usually to mid height, so he can't pull himself out of the crib. Then there's that shocking morning that your baby is standing in the crib and you haven't lowered the mattress to the lowest setting. You're ecstatic that your baby can now stand, and horrified that he could have pulled himself over the side. You will generally have to adjust the height only twice while he's in his crib, but the easier, the better. Trust me, you'll be tired.

Why was a drawer under the crib important? Baby stuff seems to multiply. We were tight on space when we had Sidney, so the draw under the crib was a must. After we renovated the house and had more room, the drawer was still packed.

Crib Mattress

Remember that beautiful four-poster bed you bought? It didn't come with a mattress, did it? Well, neither does your crib. The most important feature in a baby's mattress is that it's waterproof to withstand things like leaky diapers or spit up. Yes, there's a difference between spit up and throw-up, having mainly to do with volume. The mattress must also be firm for your baby. The one we bought had a softer side to use when it's a toddler bed. Thinking back, I'm pretty sure I couldn't tell the difference between the two sides. And contrary to what you might think, it's important that baby has a firm mattress. Too soft and he can smother himself when he's sleeping on his tummy.

Crib Tent (to Keep the Cat, Toys, and Other Odds and Ends Out)

Sidney loves her little sister. And Ellie loves her baby brother. It's really is a beautiful thing. However, they have different approaches to nurturing. We have a beautiful picture of the girls meeting Calvin in the hospital right after he was born. Sidney is leaning over to kiss him. Ellie's hand is a blur as she reaches for his nose (she thought it was a toy). When, they shared a room it was so touching to listen on the monitor as Sidney sang a fussy Ellie to sleep. What we feared was that Sidney would try to comfort Ellie by giving her a big stuffed animal or tossing a soft blanket into the crib. While this is a nice sentiment, we were just a tad concerned that it might make it a little hard for Ellie to breathe. Or, perhaps, Sidney will share her favorite book. Bonk! In addition, there is also the real possibility that the cat, if you have one, might want to cuddle up with a soft warm baby. This is not that unusual.

All this (paranoia) led us to get a crib tent, which has two flexible plastic ribs that form two arches in the form of an "X." Attached to the ribs is something similar to mosquito netting. The ribs attach to the corners of the crib. Assembly was a little tricky, but once completed the front panel could be zipped open for easy access to Baby.

Bumper and Skirt

Crib bumpers are soft pads about eight to ten inches tall that wrap around the inside of the crib so your little angel won't bonk her head or arms on the hard sides of the crib. Crib skirts, like bed skirts, go under the mattress and hide the empty space under the crib and give the dust bunnies a place to breed. This gets a little into the more personal, decorating, end of things because it's your choice whether you want either of them for your nursery. When we were shopping we happened upon a bumper, skirt, and receiving blanket made by a woman named Nava. You can view products and find a store at www.navasdesigns.com. Once we saw her products everything else paled by comparison. It took some major soul-searching to justify the expense, but we are extremely happy with what we got. However, looking back, we totally overspent. The bumper was only used for a few months, and the skirt covered the drawer, so we didn't use it (the skirt, that is). And the receiving blanket? It was received by a wooden rod that displayed it on the wall of the nursery. We hung it on the wall where we looked at it for the entire time our children were infants. Now it's stored away for grandkids.

Note: make sure to check the latest research on the use of bumpers. Things had changed by the time we had Calvin and we saw recommendations against putting them in cribs because they can restrict air movement.

Changing Table

When we did our research we found that there are two basic kinds of changing tables: flat and two-tiered. The flat ones are just that, flat, although some have raised sides. They tend to have three drawers their full width. Tiered changing tables have an upper section about one quarter of its width raised about six inches above the area where the changing pad goes. This is ideal for putting lotions, diapers and wipes, or whatever was in your hand when you picked up Baby to change her. It also got those products out of the way of our extremely active, kicking children who would have no doubt kicked it all onto the floor had the table been one height. The two-tiered ones have a compartment with shelves and a door under the upper tier. This was great for storing diapers, bulk baby wipes, and Diaper Genie refills. (See *Diaper Pale* under **Stuff for Keeping Clean**.) Under the changing pad side there were three drawers. We chose a two-tiered changing table for the nursery because we liked the extra storage space. I think the top drawer, to this day, still has baby junk in it.

Secondary Changing Stations

Secondary changing stations are more about need and/or convenience than they are a type of furniture. As with any backup system, it is not unusual for these to be less substantial than the primary changing table. Since we lived on more than one level it was nice to have an additional place to change our kids' diapers without having to use the floor or walk back to the nursery every time. Ours was not as fancy as the one in the nursery, but great to have. Although it was the flat type, an important feature was that the sides were raised about six inches so the kids couldn't roll off it. We also got a handy plastic bin, called a Diaper Depot, that hung over the side of the changing table to hold diapers, wipes and lotion.

Changing Table Pads and Covers

Just like a crib doesn't come with a mattress, the changing tables won't come with a pad. There are two basic kinds of pads: flat or with curved sides. For our main changing table we chose a curved pad. The kids loved it. It hugged their sides and made them feel secure when they were being changed. I'm sure it kept them from rolling off more than once. If your changing table doesn't have raised sides, make sure to attach the pad to the table so it won't slide off. Some pads come with a "seatbelt," which is good for holding Baby so she won't roll off.

Changing table pad covers are what sheets are to mattresses. They generally come in a variation of terry cloth. Make sure you get covers that fit the shape of the pad. Right after Sidney was born we realized we only had one changing pad cover, so I ventured out to get extras. I think I got fifty of them. We never had to buy another one, through three kids. It was a tiny bit of new dad overkill. And by "tiny," I mean way too much.

Glider (It's a Chair) with Gliding Footrest

This alternative to the basic rocking chair is a very helpful whether your wife is breastfeeding or not. These chairs do exactly what the name implies: glide. The base, or feet, stays put but the chair itself can gently glide back and forth in a horizontal motion, which is very comfortable. You can get them with such features as a reclining back and a lever that locks them into any point along the glide. I loved the reclining feature. It was great for leaning back and rocking Sidney to sleep. I never used the lever lock. Ours also had pockets on the sides of the arms. These were great for magazines and, believe it or not, mirrors. When I was trying to get Sidney down to sleep, I couldn't see her face, and moving her would wake her, so I kept a mirror in each pocket to see if she'd fallen asleep. Why each arm? No matter which shoulder she fell asleep on, I didn't have to reach across my body to get to a pocket/mirror on the other side.

As an accessory to the glider, you can purchase a gliding footrest. It's really amazing sitting with your feet up, and not having to bend your knees to glide back and forth. Some of these have the added feature of a pull-out platform that angles down toward the ground, similar to what the shoe salesman puts your feet on, and stops the footrest from moving. My wife said this was very helpful when breastfeeding.

We made the mistake of choosing a natural off-white cotton fabric. What were we thinking? Light-colored furniture and babies don't go together. Think pureed carrot puke. Our chair was so dirty after a year we had to have the carpet cleaners fix it. I recommend a pattern that doesn't show every splotch.

Co-sleepers and Bassinets

For the first several days, if not weeks, of your baby's life you may want her to sleep in your bedroom with you. She'll be up every two hours to feed and you'll want her close. One way to do this is to have bassinet in your bedroom. Bassinets are basically small cribs. Ours had wheels, which made it easy to move around on the hardwood floors. It had rocking-chair like rails on the bottom so when the wheels flipped up it could rock side-to-side. Never once did we use this feature. It also had a canopy, a basket underneath that was great to store extra sheets and blankets, and a vibrating device. The canopy was useful for keeping the bedroom lights out of Baby's eyes. You may only use the bassinet for about two months. So it shouldn't need the same durability as the travel crib or highchair. If you are planning on using it for a long time and want something special, try shopping at a boutique.

Be careful with the use of the vibrating device. As your child grows you are basically teaching her everything about living, and sleeping. If you use the vibrator to get her to sleep in the first days of life, she may need it for a long time to be able to sleep. Everything you use to put your baby to sleep in, such as the crib, car seat, travel crib, and the crib at Grandma's house, may therefore need to have one.

Co-sleepers are similar to bassinets, only they have one side missing. They are intended to be put against your bed, so your baby is close and easy to reach if she fusses. Make sure to compare the height of any one you're considering to the height of your bed. We had a really thick mattress that made the bed too high to work with a co-sleeper. Sandy said she would have preferred this to a bassinet.

Moses Basket

These beautiful woven baskets have a soft lining and are made to carry your newborn around. The basket is just about 30 inches long and has two handles that you can slide your arm through. We didn't have one for Sidney, but coveted our sister-in-law's and got one for Ellie. Sandy used it religiously to carry Ellie and Calvin around.

Highchair

You will start using the highchair once your baby can sit up on his own and he is eating solid food. This is usually around four to six months of age. You will probably continue to use it until your child is about two years old, maybe even three. When he is a baby and you're spoon feeding him, you'll want the chair up higher. However, once he starts feeding himself, you may want to be able to lower it so he can join you at the table and, perhaps, not use the tray. If this is the case, you'll want a highchair that is fairly adjustable. You also want good, locking castors, because it gets moved from place to place a lot.

We wanted a highchair that would last through three kids and chose one of high quality with many features. Highchairs fall into the same quality categories as the strollers, so there is a range of prices. Like portable highchairs, your highchair will get very nasty over time. It's important that the cover can come off for cleaning. I would therefore <u>not</u> recommend a chair with a cloth cover. One thing to consider is whether the tray height is adjustable. Ours was a little high for a newborn and Ellie looked like mini-me the first time we put her in it. The feature we loved best was that the seat reclined. Sidney, like her mother before her, would go until she dropped, which was usually halfway through her meal. Being able to recline the seat so she could sleep comfortably was priceless.

Chapter Ten - Everything You Never Wanted to Know About Breastfeeding but Were Afraid to Ask

Sandy decided well before we had kids that she was going to breastfeed. That alleviated the need to do heavy research on brands of formula. What I didn't realize until I started to write this book was how much information I had absorbed about storing, thawing, transporting, and using breast milk.

Breastfeeding v. Formula

Whether or not to breastfeed is one of the fundamental choices your wife must make when you have a baby. There's a tremendous amount of research that shows how good it is for your baby. Our kids were fed exclusively breast milk until they started on solid food at about one year of age. Many of the people I work with said they didn't breastfeed because it was too much work. This didn't make sense to us because if Mom is around, there's nothing to prepare. However, in writing this, I realize there are many steps to go through if you're going to be prepared to pump, store, and use breast milk. But to breastfeed, all your wife needs is a little privacy, or not. Many women have no issue throwing a blanket over their shoulder and feeding Baby wherever they may be. If Dad is alone with the baby he has to prepare a meal for her, why not breast milk? (No silly, you store Mom's in the fridge.) It's easy, and it's what Mother Nature intended. That said, it is sometimes difficult for Mom if she has to go back to work because she has to pump and store, and sometimes this can get a little painful. But research shows that a little breastfeeding is better than none. There are some really good formulas available. Check with your pediatrician on what he recommends. Whether to use them as a supplement or as the only food depends on your personal choice. One thing I will warn you about, and this has nothing to do with your baby, is that you, the man, will probably lose dibs on that part of your wife's body because during the months she is breastfeeding they are property of the baby.

Bottles and Bottle Starter Kits

I remember staring at the bottle display in the store for hours (okay, a few minutes) totally confused by all the choices. I think I ultimately bought one of everything. The science and hoopla behind the various brands is staggering. What it comes down to is that newborns need bottles with a very slow flow that won't let in a lot of air. So make sure you get stage one, or slow-flow nipples. If the milk flows too fast your baby may gag on it. You may be given a bottle starter kit for your baby, but don't be surprised if Baby rejects it, because babies are very particular when it comes to bottles. The hospital may also be giving out a brand or shape you don't like. The general advice we got was to make sure the nipple is as close to Mother Nature as possible. The other thing you are aiming for is to reduce air intake (by the baby), and therefore gas. We ultimately settled on "Vent-Air" and "Nursers," both by Playtex. The latter has collapsible disposable liners called "drop-ins." Since the liners, or bags, collapse as they're emptied, they help limit gas, and the only thing you have to clean is the nipple. We could use the bags of our stored breast milk without having to transfer the milk to another container.

One thing to be wary of if you breastfeed is "nipple confusion." Apparently, it's way easier getting milk out of a bottle than getting it out of the breast. So if you plan on doing both, we were told it's important not to start the bottle for about three weeks after birth. Once you start supplementing with a bottle I recommend you do not stop. Here's a "no one ever told me that" tidbit: if you stop using the bottle and go back exclusively to Mommy your baby may then reject the bottle. This happened to us with Sidney. We stopped using the bottle for several weeks and when we tried to go back, she would have none of it. She wanted Mommy. Period. That meant Mommy could never be away from Sidney for more than a few hours. There's a lot to be said for the closeness of breastfeeding. There's more to be said about Mom getting some time for herself and being able to go to the occasional meeting without a baby. We didn't make the same mistake with Ellie or Calvin.

Breast Pump

I realize this is not exactly something every gentleman feels he should know, because you're the Dad, the Man, the Fixer. While you won't be using it, you'll be carrying it, and you should know about spare parts. There are several reputable manufacturers of breast pumps. They come from simple hand pumps to double electric pumps. That's right, to pump both at the same time. There's a lot of personal choice here so look at websites that offer comparisons like www.breastpumpcomparisons.com or www.consumerreports.org. We landed on a "Pump in Style" by Medela. They make several versions of the electric breast pump. Ours came with two cups, affectionately known as bugles. You can also purchase a harness, which leaves your hands free and you don't have to hold the bugles. The case comes with storage for the various parts and a cold storage area, with ice packs, for storing the milk.

If you have a dog, or will be frequently visiting someone who does, we recommend getting spare parts in advance. Our dog, as sweet and well trained as she was, got ahold of the bugles and decided they were a delicacy and chewed up several of them. There are also some little plastic back-flow regulator valves that attach the bugle to the tubing. They're very important, very small and delicate, and if they break the pump won't work, so it's good to have extras around. Finding spare parts is easier said than done. Medela has a website, but they don't sell parts there. Sandy had to trek three towns over after the dog chewed the last one of the bugles, which was not fun with a newborn in tow.

If you're sure you'll only be breastfeeding for a couple of months, look into renting a pump from the hospital.

Transporting Breast Milk
There's always a lot to carry when going on a day trip with your baby. If she's breastfed and Mom's not coming along you have to bring some milk along. The first time I did this I brought the whole pump, because it has a "freezer" section.

That was a little cumbersome to carry to say the least. Not to mention that Mom may need it wherever she is. Some diaper bags have a compartment that's intended for cold storage. For us, the best solution was a small thermal shoulder bag intended for school kids' lunches. We got it at Target. It was light, compact, and frozen friendly. When we had to go to Washington, DC for a five-day conference and needed to bring a supply, this was just the thing.

Storing Breast Milk

One thing you'll learn, and probably hear repeatedly, is that breast milk is like gold. Pumping isn't fun, and if you're exclusively feeding on breast milk you want to ensure you have enough safely stored for future use. That means you're going to want to build up about a three-day supply of breast milk. That way if your wife is out, or the two of you go away for the weekend, you're all set. It's also needed for moms who are returning to work so there's a supply for Dad or the babysitter.

So, where do you store this "gold"? If you know you're going to use it right away, like the next morning for cereal (not yours, the baby's), then the fridge is the best place. You can safely keep milk in the fridge for several days, but after about

24 hours it starts to lose some of the nutrients. It loses even more nutrients in the freezer, but some things can't be helped. For storage up to a month, the freezer is the best place. If you want to go long term, up to about six months, a top-loaded freezer that's zero degrees is your best bet. More details can be found in *The Womanly Art of Breastfeeding* published by La Leche League. There is also expert advice online at Dr Sears' website at www.askdrsears.com .

Our breast pump came with handy containers to pump the milk into. Ultimately, we abandoned these in favor of plastic storage bags to save the added step of transferring the milk from the containers to the bags we stored in the freezer. We tried several brands of bags and ultimately used Gerber sterilized zip-lock bags. Since we had a bottle with disposable inserts, we used these bags in lieu of the ones that came with the bottle.

Keep a Sharpie (that's a permanent marker) handy so you can mark the date and number of ounces on each bag before you store it. You'll want the date so you can always use the oldest milk first. The quantity is useful because you won't always want the same amount. For example, you may only want two ounces for cereal and four ounces for a feeding. But if you get done with a feeding and Baby is still hungry, you'll want to use one of the smaller bags so less milk goes to waste in case she's not that hungry. Once you've thawed breast milk you shouldn't refreeze it.

When to Get the Bottle Ready

Okay, Mom's gone out and you've got this baby to feed. Do yourself a favor, don't wait till she's hungry to get a bottle ready. Been there, done that. In the ten minutes it takes to get the bottle ready, which is an eternity to a newborn, she will get herself totally upset and so worked up that she'll give herself gas. Then she may not be able to calm down to eat and it will go downhill from there. Also remember that newborns eat every two hours or so. Breast milk stays good at room temperature for about four hours, or more depending on the temperature of the room. (Meaning less in hot rooms.) Do the math and when Mom leaves, get a bottle ready. Just leave it on the counter until you start seeing hunger signs and then snuggle up with her and give her some milk. It's beautiful. And don't worry, you'll begin to recognize hunger signs after a few days of being a parent.

Thawing Breast Milk

Putting breast milk in the microwave will kill all the good stuff, so that's out. You also don't want it to get too hot or you'll burn your baby's mouth. The rule of thumb for just about anything you're feeding baby is to put a little on your forearm to see if it's the right temp. Don't just stick you're finger in it. Our grown-up fingers are calloused and not as temperature sensitive as our forearms.

So you'll need a quick way to thaw the milk without taking it out of the bag. What I found very effective was to run hot water into a glass bowl in the sink and dip the milk bag into it like a tea bag. This usually took about three minutes and let me control the temperature of the milk by feeling it through the bag on my forearm. If the milk got too hot, I simply ran cold water into the bowl, dipped a few times and, voila, I had milk ready to serve.

If you have other things to do, like get a tub ready for your other child, you can put the milk bag in the bowl and let the water run. When you do this, make sure the water is on the approximate outcome temperature you want or you'll make the milk too hot. If you do, see above.

Warming Refrigerated Breast Milk

The approach to warming refrigerated milk versus frozen milk can be completely different. We used the method above for both types for a long time and one day I woke up and thought, "Hey, we've got these bottle warmers, why don't we use them to warm a bottle?" I swear children suck the common sense out of you. If you have breast milk in the fridge and you want to warm it, the easiest way is to use a bottle warmer. If your milk is in a bag, transfer it to either a bottle or a milk/food storage jar because the bags don't interact well with the warmer. Make sure to adjust the temperature on the warmer so the milk doesn't overheat.

Another handy use for bottle warmers is to heat water for changing wipes. See **Keeping Clean** for more information.

Nothing Like a Good Burp

Whether you are nursing or bottle-feeding there are actually two goals. The first, and most obvious, is to feed the baby. The second is to limit the amount of air she swallows because it will likely turn to gas. Gas is very uncomfortable to babies. They don't understand pain, where it comes from, or how to deal with it. So gas turns into crying. The best way to avoid this is a good burp. That's why you try really hard after every feeding to get a good burp. Babies tend to swallow far less air when breastfeeding, so the risk of discomfort is far less.

Burping a baby is a balance of finesse and frustration. Place your baby's belly on your chest with her head sticking up over one of your shoulders and gently pat her back. You can vary the strength of the pats and I usually would gently rub between pats. Sooner or later you'll get a burp. However, sometimes the burps are so soft you can't hear them or they take a long time. This can lead to frustration or impatience (on Dad's part). Eventually you'll lose the novice feelings of inexperience and have the confident touch of an expert.

If she does get gas, sometimes you just have to wait it out. When she gets old enough there are some over–the-counter gas medicines in liquid form that are safe for babies. Talk to your doctor about what age you can start to use them. (See *The Short List of Medications* in **Medicine and First Aid**.)

<u>Boppy</u>

Since this book is written from a male point of view, I'm not going to presume to give advice on breastfeeding. However, there was one thing that made it much more comfortable for Sandy when the babies were small (during the first two months or so). It's called a "Boppy" and it's a U- shaped pillow that fits around Mom's waist while she's sitting. You can lay your baby on it, which frees up a hand (sometimes two) while breastfeeding. Sandy used it at the dinner table for support so she'd have a free hand to eat. It comes with a removable, washable cover that is available in many colors. I have no idea where this got its name, because you don't actually bop anyone with it. For more information about this and other products, see www.boppy.com .

As a side note, when your baby starts to sit up, but is still wobbly, these are great to "embrace" her and keep her from toppling over.

Nursing Pads

Nursing pads are for women to insert into their bra. Sometimes women produce more milk than the baby needs and they may leak. The nursing pads absorb this overage. There are special bras for nursing that allow for easy access for your baby (not you, you pig). Some of them have pockets for nursing pads.

Pacifiers

Let's think about what these actually replace. Figure it out? Sometimes your baby will use Mom's breast just as a way to calm down. I know that may sound like fun for you, but for Mom it actually can get kind of painful. We affectionately referred to these as "puckies," and if your baby is fussing and you're sure she's not hungry, because she just nursed for an hour, try putting a pacifier in her mouth. It may not only calm her down, but it may also give Mom a break. Don't have pacifier handy? You can also use your finger if it's clean.

Our kids never took to the pacifier for the long term, but it did help in the early days with Ellie. Pacifiers come in different sizes based on age so make sure you have infant pacifiers on hand. You'll also want to make sure they're BPA free (that's a kind of plastic). While there were times when we wished we could simply put a pacifier in our child's mouth to calm him down, in the long run we felt it was best not to rely on it. Because by not using a pacifier as a means of soothing, our kids learned how to self-calm. We've seen and heard stories of parents trying to wean their kids from pacifiers or their thumbs up through age four and we're very grateful we didn't have to go through that.

Chapter Eleven - Stuff for Eating

At first all your baby will eat is breast milk or formula. He will not be on anything "solid" for at least four, maybe six, months unless your doctor tells you otherwise. By "solid" I mean soupy, pasty mush. Once he starts on solid food there is a growing debate on what is the best first food. So check with your doctor.

One of the reasons feeding a baby food is so messy is that children have a built-in reflex to push anything in their mouth out with their tongue. Eating solids is a learned skill. Our kids had this reaction, but once they got the hang of solid food they couldn't get it fast enough. This was, no doubt, inherited from their mother due to her general lack of patience. Alright it was really from me because, I'm told, I did exactly the same thing and fussed between spoonfuls. (By the way, expect that every time your child does something bad it's "your" son, but when he's an angel, he's definitely your wife's.) There are a lot of ways to feed your baby once he starts on "solids." The generally accepted way is one spoonful at a time. However, we learned something from Sidney when she was fussing to get her cereal. I put the bowl to her lips and she literally sucked down the cereal. We learned something else from Ellie, put the cereal in a sippy cup, take out the rubber stopper thingy, and it's much less messy. This also helped overcome the pushing-it-out-of-the-mouth reflex. But be warned, this may not be for everyone as the cereal will come out fast and may be a choking hazard.

Cereal

When Sandy first told me the first solid food we'd be giving Sidney was cereal, I thought she'd gone mad. Cereal to me was Frosted Flakes. "No silly, it's rice flakes (almost like powder) you mix with breast milk (or water)." It comes in regular and organic.

Two tips. One: You know how if you leave your oatmeal in the bowl for a while it gets thicker, almost like glue? Baby cereal does the opposite. It gets thinner. Maybe someday I'll get a physicist-type person to explain this to me, but for now, keep the box handy, because if it gets too thin it's hard to feed. Two: Keep a baby bottle filled with water handy. Sometimes he may just need to wash it down. Think about it, have you ever tried to eat a whole bowl of oatmeal with nothing to drink?

"Solid" Food

At about six months or so your doctor will tell you it's okay to start your baby on "baby" food, AKA mush. I recommend that you start with the vegetables. If you start with fruits, she'll get used to the sweetness and may never want the veggies. Our doctor recommended that we start one new food every three days. That way if she has a reaction you'll know to which food. For that reason, it's also a good idea to start her on new foods in the morning or at lunch. If she's going to have a reaction, better to have it during the day than at night. And keep a baby bottle filled with water handy in case she gets thirsty.

One more thing, once you give her a spoonful and put the spoon back in the jar, you're done. You either have to finish the jar or throw it away. It's a germ thing. So if you think she may not be up to a whole jar, put some in a bowl. You can always take more out (with a clean spoon), then throw the jar in the fridge for later. But be careful heating it up again, especially if it's with a microwave. A half-full jar will heat up very quickly, so make sure to stir and test the temperature to avoid burning that little mouth.

Spoons

Baby spoons come in a variety of sizes and colors. Keep a lot on hand. Once you start on solid food, you'll go through as many as eight to ten every day. They pretty much all have a plastic covering on the spoon end (as opposed to metal). What I found really neat about baby spoons was that with some brands the end changes color, to white, if the food is too hot. It's still a good idea to test the temperature of the food just to be sure. I found a brand that had extra-long handles, which were good for grown-up hands. They had a deep spoon area that could hold more food, and they were kind of flexible, which made squeegeeing the food off baby's face more efficient and (probably) more comfortable. There are also spoons with hollow handles that you can put a few ounces of food into and squeeze it out as you need it. Naturally these arrived on the market after our kids were done with baby food.

Bowls

Babies are fascinated with gravity, so a lot of things end up on the floor. It is important, therefore, to have a lot of nonbreakable stuff (and a dog) around. This applies especially to bowls, plates, and cups.

Baby bowls come in many shapes and sizes. Some are divided into two or three sections. This is particularly handy when he starts baby food and you want to feed two different foods at once. Think about it, how often do you eat a meal and only have one thing? (Cheese steaks [It's a Philly thing] don't count.) When he graduates to table food, you'll want bowls with non-slip bottoms. We found some with suction cups to hold them down. Kids have this natural tendency to use their arms as windshield wiper, which sends stuff flying. Suction cups should reduce the number of bowls that hit the ground. Some bowls have a horizontal lip around the edge, but we preferred ones with a plain edge for when our impatient little eaters wanted their food shoveled.

Cups

A sippy cup has a screw-on lid and a little spout that enables your child to drink liquids without your aid and without spilling. In addition to only having a small slit in the mouthpiece, the good ones have a plastic insert that goes inside the lid. This prevents water or juice from seeping out when they are knocked over, dropped, or generally left lying around. To get anything out of them your baby has to suck pretty hard. We had some less intricate ones that only had the slit in the mouthpiece. These worked marginally well for regular drinks, but were good for thicker drinks like milkshakes. Another step down the sippy cup evolutionary scale are cups with a small hole in the lid. We affectionately called these drippy cups because they only slow the slippage down to a slow gush. They also come in a disposable version and are handy as your child gets more competent handling his own drink. Eventually he will graduate to a "big boy cup," also known as a plastic cup.

The cabinet we kept all these in looked like a sippy cup junk yard. There was a ragtag of mismatched cups and lids. Ultimately we landed on one brand that worked well for us and were able to combine all the spare parts into a usable assortment. Don't be surprised if for several years you find sippy cups with fermented juice in the most inopportune places like in or under the couch, between the car seats, etc. Those you may want to simply throw away because I think the mold gets permanently attached to the plastic.

Chapter Twelve - Clothing, Stuff to Wear

One thing to keep in mind about any baby clothing is that it should be permanent-press machine washable. I don't care how fashion-conscious you are, you don't want to have to iron it. When you have a baby you will be doing more laundry than you ever imagined. The general rule is, the smaller they are, the more dirty clothes and diapers there will be. You definitely don't want to dry clean your baby's clothing. For one, it's expensive, but more important, I think it's a bad idea to have those harsh chemicals next to your baby's skin.

There is also special, extra-mild laundry detergent for baby's clothing. Dreft and Ivory both come to mind. All baby clothes should be washed in this for the first year. Sleepwear should not have any fabric softener, as that could make it more flammable.

The Size Mystery

You'll find that there is a mystery to sizing baby stuff. I think the same people who decided to make all women's clothing run large, so women can brag about how small their bodies are, got together and decided all baby clothes should run small, so parents can brag about how big their kids are. Our kids were always in the next size up.

Read the tag carefully. In addition to small, medium, large designations, it will give the size in several other ways: age, height, and/or weight. You can usually ignore the whole age thing. Make sure the clothes you buy fit the length and weight of your baby and you'll make out okay. How will you know the length and weight of your baby? Believe me when I say that these vital statistics get etched into your brain. They're discussion points and bragging rights. The second question everyone will ask you when you tell them you just had a baby is "How big?"

The Dressing Rule of Thumb

Are you comfortable in the clothes you're wearing right now? Your baby will generally be comfortable in one more layer than you wear. By one more layer, I'm not referring to an overcoat. I simply mean that if you're wearing a T-shirt, he should have on two. Newborns lack the ability to self-regulate body temperature, so you need to pay special attention to his clothes when at that age.

Body Suits – AKA Onesies

Technically speaking, the term "Onesie" is trademarked by Gerber. It has become synonymous with baby clothes the way Kleenex has with tissues. A "Onesie" is generally a one-piece T-shirt that snaps under the crotch and also comes in long-sleeve versions for colder weather. They should always be 100% cotton. In hot weather a T-shirt Onesie may be all you need. When it's cold you can throw on a shirt and pants over them and Baby's good to go. We started with ones made by Gerber and also came to love the ones made by Gap and Oshkosh along the way. These were somewhat thicker and also very soft. Regardless of the brand, have enough of these on hand to change baby a few times a day. More if she has a tendency to spit up a lot.

Sleepers

I have this image of my two year old walking around in a purple fleece sleeper with padded rubber feet clutching the stuffed toy monkey we got at the zoo. The sleeper had a zipper from the top of her right foot to just under her chin. Starting from the time she is born you can put your baby in a sleeper. There are many definitions of a sleeper: some have feet, some don't; some are light cotton, some are heavy fleece. It all depends on the time of year and your preference. At some point during her second year, Sidney started wearing pajamas. You know, two pieces, bottoms and tops. That was traumatic for her mom. It meant she was growing up.

In general you want to make sure any sleeper you get doesn't have any snaps in the back. This is because babies always should be put to bed on their backs, and the snaps can be uncomfortable. One of the mantras you'll hear is: "Put your baby 'back' to sleep," unless the research changes and the American Academy of Pediatrics changes its recommendation. Also, pay attention to the temperature in the house. If you're sleeping with the air-conditioning on, your baby may get cold in a lightweight cotton sleeper, even though it's summer. Check with your doctor but you probably won't be covering him with a blanket until he's about eight months old. Even then if he's active in his sleep he may just kick it off. So you'll want his evening-wear to be temperature appropriate.

SIDS Sleepers

SIDS stands for Sudden Infant Death Syndrome. Not something anyone ever wants to know about firsthand. SIDS sleepers are basically zip-up sacks you can put your baby in to sleep at night. I prefer to call them sleeping sacks. On cold nights a heavy sleeper may not be enough and we didn't want to risk putting a blanket in the crib, so a sleeping sack was the solution. If you can't find one in the store, there are plenty of places online like www.target.com or www.comfykid.com where you can buy them.

There are a lot of hypothesis about what causes SIDS, but no one knows for sure. It is believed to have to do with breathing issues with small babies. For that reason it is important not to put anything on the baby or in the crib that could interfere with nighttime breathing. I believe that small infants lack some of the self-defense reflexes that older babies or adults do.

Receiving Blankets

These are named literally for receiving the baby when someone passes her to you. They have a plethora of uses in addition to lightly wrapping your newborn when you're holding him or passing him to a friend. They can also be used for making baby burritos (see *Gas Relief via Swaddling* in the **Parenting Tips – Stuff About Baby** section). They go over your shoulder when he's sleeping on you. You use them as privacy cover if you're wife is breastfeeding in public. Put them down over the changing station in a public bathroom (because the station may be dirty and you don't want Baby touching it [and make sure you wash the blanket before you use it again]). They come in cotton, fleece, flannel, etc. Get a variety. You'll need them for all seasons.

Bibs – Zillions of Them

Bibs are like baseball caps. You can find them with virtually anything printed on them. They come in many sizes and colors. Most bibs are cotton. Some have plastic-coated backs so the food/liquid doesn't soak through. That's okay, but not a must. They come with Velcro "clasps," snaps, ties, or pull-over. We liked the Velcro the best. Ties are less convenient and can be hard to get off if you're putting him down for a nap. You'll go through bibs like water, so have a lot on hand.

Babies tend to drool, just 'cause. There's so much to put in their little mouths, it's mouthwatering. Unless you want to change his clothes every two hours, have him wear a bib. Once a baby gets into the habit of life without drooling, he starts all over again because he's teething. So you'll have to break out the bibs for that too. Oh yeah, and babies dribble, drool, and spit when they eat. Okay, maybe they don't spit, but you'll want him to wear a bib during meals. For eating "solid" baby food you may want to get some larger bibs or over-sized, pull-over bibs. These are great for keeping him clean(er) so you don't trash his outfit.

When he's eating table food, you can get the plastic bibs with pockets at the bottom. This will stop about 11% of the food he drops from hitting the floor. (A highly scientific observation.)

Socks

One thing we still don't understand is why the newborn socks we bought had non-slip pads on the bottom. Where's she going to go? We started our baby-stuff buying careers shopping at Babies-R-Us and socks were no exception. It was a good start, but when Sidney got older we needed another source because she went through socks quickly. Old Navy had a good selection of baby/toddler socks, and they were very affordable. Many had rubberized netting or bumps on the bottom, and when your baby is first starting to walk, this is important. Every little bit helps keep her on her feet. We were also happy with the selection and quality of the socks at The Gap. We found that sport socks with short sides stayed on great. If there's one message here it's **get lots of the same socks**. You do know that washing machines are specially designed to eat one sock out of every pair, right? So if you buy lots of the same sock, the machine can get its food and you can still have matching socks. Okay, the washing machine part is a joke, but the need for lots of the same sock is not.

Hats

These fall into three general categories: infant, winter, and sun.

1. Infant hats are soft and warm. You should keep your baby's head covered most of the time for about the first two weeks of life. Double check this with your doctor. This is especially important when he's sleeping so he doesn't lose a lot of heat through his head and get cold. Buy some soft hats before you have your baby and bring them to the hospital. The best hat you'll get is the one they put on the baby right after he's born. He's all covered in goop, so the hat gets goopy. Then they clean him up, give him a shampoo and let you pick from a pile of really ugly ones (hats that is.) Sandy tells me I picked the ugliest hat in the hospital for Sidney. If you have animals, it's a good idea to hang onto the goopy hat. Bring it home with you, or send it home with a relative and let your cat or dog sniff it, before you come home with your newborn. This will give your animal a chance to get used to the new smell. Under no circumstances should you let

your animal use the hat as plaything. That smell needs to be cherished and protected, not batted around.

2. Winter hats are obviously meant to keep your baby's head warm when she's outside in the cold. When you first put them on, babies have a tendency to pull them off so you may want to consider getting ones with a chin strap.

3. Sun hats: Baby's skin is extremely sensitive so you should put a hat on whenever you have her outside in the sun. As with winter hats, you may want to try one with a chin strap. For girls there are all sorts of frilly, flowery, wide brim hats you can buy. For boys, they make baby-sized ball caps. Remember, if you use one of these, his ears and the back of his neck are not protected from the sun.

Chapter Thirteen - Stuff for Playing

There is nothing more fun and enjoyable than playing with your baby. Okay, well maybe that thing you did that caused you to have the baby in the first place, but I digress. With just about any toy you play with you are also teaching her something new. Some research suggests you don't need fancy toys for your baby to learn and that a metal bowl and wooden spoon will suffice. I believe that's true, but it can get rather noisy. One of the things you want to teach your baby is how to play by herself. At first this may only amount to about two minutes. But that's all the time you need to give your arms a break.

By the way, all those lovely pastel toys: your baby can't see them. Well, that is to say, he can't see the colors. You baby's vision develops slowly. At first he can only see about eight to ten inches. At four months he can focus on objects about three feet away. All this time he can really only see high-contrast bright colors. Keep this in mind when you're shopping for those early toys.

Thick Blankets for Playing on the Floor

When you have a baby, a lot of your time is spent on the floor. Babies need to be stimulated and played with and a lot of that is done when they are lying down. No matter how much of a neat freak you are, your floor in going to get, or be, dirty. You also may want to play with your baby outside, or at a friend's house. You can use a thick receiving blanket for this. You also may want to get some larger, thick, soft blankets or quilts.

Activity Centers

I've broken the playthings section down into two basic parts: play toys and activity centers. Play toys are just what they sound like, toys. See **Play Toys – A Few of My Favorite Things** below. Activity centers are things like swings and jumpers that your baby can play in or on.

Bouncy Seat

This is a seat in a sling on a metal frame that allows your baby to gently bounce up and down. They are generally not meant for use until she is holding up her head. Ours had a canopy, which I didn't like, and a crossbar with some toys, which I did. It also had a console with a vibrator and music maker. Neither of our children really took to this seat, but a colleague of mine said his son loved it.

As an alternative, we got a "travel" bouncy seat. Instead of a metal frame, it had heavy plastic rocking chair–type "rails." It didn't really rock that well, but it had two straps we could use to easily lift the whole seat, baby included, and carry her around. Since she was in an upright position we didn't have to worry as much about spit up. To make it even more conducive to sleep, we attached a crib vibrator to it. We also used it for feedings when we were away from the highchair. The cover came off for easy cleaning.

<u>Baby Swing</u>

For some reason, babies love rocking, whether it's in your arms, in a glider, or in a swing. These small quad-pod supported swings are more for entertaining than playing. Meaning they help you retain your sanity by safely putting baby down so you can get some alone time, or other baby time if you've got more than one at home. Using a swing was one of the few ways we could get Sidney down for a nap.

We bought one with every bell and whistle, and got more than we needed. It had six speed settings, music that played at three volumes, and a timer with three settings. We used the speed settings all the time. I never used the music, but Sandy used it quite a bit. We never used the timer. It also came with a mobile for baby to look up at that was quickly removed and lost.

When shopping for a swing the most important feature is that it's completely open at the top so it's easy to get your Baby in and out.

Jumper

Boing, boing, boing. Most babies love to bounce. That's why someone invented the "Jolly Jumper." It hooks over the top of most door jambs. It has a height-adjustable, spring-loaded sitting harness that lets your baby's feet just touch the ground, making him feel fairly weightless when he bounces up in the air. If you live in a house with really large trim, like we did, the hooks may not fit over your door jambs. So we improvised to make it work. Sidney loved the swing. Ellie was a maybe. Calvin was indifferent. Kids are all *so* different

Swing – Outdoor (Indoor)

In the spring, after Sidney turned one, we got a toddler swing for outside and hooked it to the porch beam. She loved it. Then came winter and boredom set in. I made a minor adjustment to the jumper adapter I had built so we could attach the swing indoors. We had fun all winter. Being an architect and carpenter, I am confident in the things I build. However, you should use extreme caution when modifying your house to work with various toys, as this is not for everyone.

Sidney's favorite game in the swing was pretending it was a rollercoaster. I'd pull her forward to horizontal saying, "click, click, click, click." The higher she got, the bigger the smile. Then I'd let go and say "weeeeee." Two years later Sidney would go over to Ellie when she was in her baby swing and pull her forward and saying "click, click, click, wee." It's amazing what kids pick up.

Entertainment Center

This is a large, three-foot diameter, plastic doughnut, held up by three spring-loaded adjustable legs with a sling in the middle of it that she can "stand" in. All around the doughnut are toys for your baby to play with. Because of the springs the legs have a little give in them for when she bounces up and down. Once your baby can keep her head up this is a great place to put her for five to twenty minutes of play. It was a "go to" thing for us to get a few minutes to eat dinner. The toys on it range from rings she can move back and forth to a little keyboard that plays songs. The sling rotates so she can choose different toys and/or follow you around the room. Because her feet are touching the base, and there's some adjustability in the supports, it also helps build leg strength. Using interlocking chain links we also attached various teething toys. There are countless versions of these and I have to say that this was one case where buying one with all the bells and whistles was worth it. About the only feature we never used was the option to convert it to a toddler play center by opening up the doughnut. By the time Sidney was toddling we had so many other toys that this was stored safely away in the basement for the next baby.

Play Mat and Gymini

You need to give your baby some "belly" time to play. Belly time is supervised time when an infant is on the floor on his belly. This gives him a chance to develop his arms and upper back and learn to roll over. Play mats give him something to do other than stare at the floor. They have pieces with different textures and colors that make different sounds.

A spin-off of the mat has two arches that you can hang toys from that he can reach for and play with when he's on his back. This is affectionately known as a Gymini. It helps develop hand-eye coordination and gives him stuff to pull at and put in his mouth. To babies, everything in the world must be tasted. There are a slew of additional toys you can buy/hang. We added toys as we found cool (read colorful) ones and attached them mainly with chain links. Since both these thing live on the ground they require frequent washing.

Crib Mobile

These attach to the crib and rotate and play music to keep your baby entertained. Believe it or not, the best one for your baby is probably the ugliest one you see. Remember, they need contrasting colors and you need to think of things from your baby's perspective. We got one with electric blue, neon green, and glowing magenta monkeys on it. It clashed with everything. As it rotated, the monkeys moved around a cone at the end of each arm. The bottom of the cones had black and white swirls. It was completely gaudy, but it kept the kids' attention when they were first lying in their crib.

We got a mobile made by TinyLove called "Symphony in Motion." When we brought it out of storage for Ellie, our second child, we couldn't find the large plastic nut that holds it to the crib. After emailing them the serial number, they sent us a new part, free of charge.

<u>Play Toys - A Few of My Favorite Things.</u>
There are a ton of different kinds of toys for babies and toddlers. It would be impossible for me describe every single one. However, there are some that we just loved, couldn't live without, or just think are cool. I used to spend a bundle on toys for my cat. It turned out his favorite thing was a tiny wad of crumbled paper. The thing about toys is you don't have to spend a bundle for your children to learn and/or have fun and teach them imagination.

Sometimes when I visit people's houses I am amazed by the sheer quantity of toys they have for their baby. I swore I would never have that many toys in my house, but to no avail. My problem is that architects hate clutter. As parents, we are, no doubt, part of the clutter problem. How hard is it to walk by a cool puzzle, stuffed animal, or game and not want to buy it for the kids. Grandparents add to the problem too. Let's face it, if this is my worst problem, I have no problems.

But First the Clutter - Toy Bins

To combat the ever-growing number of toys, objects, crayons, beads, and stuffed animals (I swear they multiply at night), I suggest you do two things. First, place toy bins throughout the house. Even the rooms that aren't designated play areas, if there is such a thing, can benefit from having a small container in the corner to throw the toys in when you clean up. We didn't do that in the living room and about once a week I went in there, blew my whistle and told the toys to march back to the play room. (No, I don't really have a whistle. I've also found the toys very hard to train.)

Toy bins come in all shapes and sizes and can be purchased from a variety of sources. We got some rolling drawers from Pottery Barn Kids that slid under a play table. They hold a lot of stuff and slide away out of view. We found an expandable mesh bin at Ikea. When it's empty it crunches down to almost nothing and can be stored in a closet. In the playroom we had an assortment of baskets for tossing the toys in for cleanup. We also found some stackable compartments from Target. One thing to be careful of is if you get a bin with a top, make sure that there is an open center at the top of the sides so little fingers are less likely to get pinched. Also, be careful if you get one with a sealable lid. When Calvin was three, he thought it would be really cool to lie down in it and have his playmate seal him up. That lid is still in the basement.

Second, every two to six months you should rotate the toys. This doesn't mean turn them in the sunlight so they grow evenly, believe me, nothing stops them from growing. It means putting away the ones that don't get much use, or that your son is bored with and weeding out the ones that are no longer age appropriate. Take an old toy out in two months and it's like getting a new one. It's a good theory but it can be quite time consuming and we were never that great at it. When we did get to it we had less clutter and, believe it or not, happier kids. Just be sure they're not watching when you do it or that toy you're putting away is the one he was "just about to play with."

Toys for Tubby Time

You will be spending a good deal of time in the bathroom with, or washing, your baby from infancy to well past the toddler years. I'm sure there are many names people call giving their kids a bath. We call it Tubby Time. As a grown up, if you like to take baths you may be content to stare at the wall. However, my wife never takes a tub without something to read. Kids are no different. So to make it interesting, it's good to have a few, or maybe many, toys for your toddler to play with. It's also a good idea to have a place to store them. The toys we used regularly went into a net that stuck to the wall of the tub with suction cups. We kept a plastic bin under the sink to store the toys we rotated in and out of the tub.

From floating islands with water slides, to Barbie dolls, to Hot Wheels, to plastic dinosaurs, there is no end to the toys kids will play with in the tub. We got a lot of use out of spongy numbers and letters that float and can be stuck to the wall of the tub. Before she learned what they meant, Sidney started identifying the colors. For a while we used tub crayons, which are water soluble. These were great for drawing wash-away pictures on the wall of the tub, but we ultimately shied away from them because they stained the grout. Be wary of hollow plastic toys, like little animals, with a tiny hole in the bottom. Water gets into these and breeds mold and other yuckies, and they're impossible to clean.

With all these options, when she was a toddler, Sidney's favorite tubby toy was two little plastic cups she could use to pour water back and forth. It's a perfect example of how you don't have to spend a lot of money for your child to have fun and learn. Of course, it was always a little challenging to keep the water in the tub. But she learned cause and effect, and if she wasn't making a mess, she wasn't being a kid.

Baby Einstein Movies

These movies were developed especially for infants. The company is now owned by Disney but was developed by a mom who wanted to help her kids learn and grow. They have a variety of thirty-minute videos with different themes targeted at children from three months to three years. These are a great way to catch twenty minutes of "you" time while not feeling too guilty about putting your baby in front of cartoons. At press time these were only available as DVDs and have the added feature of letting you set them on automatic repeat.

If you're a research junkie like my wife, you'll note that there was a study done in 2007 that suggested that these kinds of videos were bad for children. You will also see that a year later there were other studies published that said the videos were neither good nor bad for children. It's a common conundrum that you can find research to support either side of an argument. We liked the videos but you'll have to decide for yourself.

Crib Entertainer

This kind of resembled a TV screen you strap into the crib. Only it didn't play any movies; it was more like a live show. The version we had attached with a strap and was reversible with the two sides addressing different developmental stages. It had lots of colorful bells, whistles, buttons, pulls, and spinners. There were reversible feet, and they actually looked like feet, that held it steady and off the mattress so our babies could play with it. It was great for the early months when the kids were lying down, but also great after they could sit up.

Lots of Little Toys

One of the first things your baby will learn to do is grab things. Then he'll want to put everything in his mouth. This may seem simple, but it's actually kind of complex. First, he has to learn to see. Remember, your baby can't see colors for about two to four months. Then he has to track things with his eyes. Then judge distance. Last, master the basic function of gripping and holding. Having a lot of little toys with high contrast, varying texture, and that make different noises is a great way to stimulate his motor skills and keep him entertained. Make sure to get some with dangling things, like feet that he can pull on and put in his mouth. None of the toys should be small enough to fit through a toilet paper tube or they're a choking hazard.

You'll also notice that many of the larger small toys have little loops on their backs. This makes them ideal for attaching to your Gymini, Bjorn (harness), or car seat using "chain links" (see below). Toys made by Lamaze epitomize what we look for in baby toys. They are multi-textured, multicolored, and many have dangly things for baby to pull on and chew. We also came to love toys made by Sassy.

Chain Links

Babies have a habit of dropping things. This can be from distraction, lost interest, or the simple inability to hold on. Imagine taking a walk with your baby. She's holding a little play toy and suddenly she lets it go, sending it onto the floor. This may be fine at home, but what about in a restaurant, or the beach, or when you're driving someplace? A handy, safe way to keep these little toys within arms reach is through the use of what I call baby chains. Technically they are referred to simply as links. These plastic ovals come in a variety of colors and textures. You can find them in solid colors and with patterns of black and white mixed with the colors. The textured ones have bumps and ridges, making them interesting to chew. They come in packages of ten to twelve. We probably had about fifty of them lying around at any given time. When Ellie was fussing I could give her one to gnaw on or just hold. You can link them together in varying lengths and attach them to her toys. That way, when they fall, they don't hit the ground.

Note: You can also get them shaped like the letters of the alphabet. I thought they were kind of cool, but ultimately decided they aren't that practical and don't work that well as "chain." Besides, there are better ways to teach the alphabet, and by the time she can understand letters she'll be well away from the chain gang.

Teething Beads

The version of these we had looked like a small necklace with colorful beads that were about one-half inch in diameter and one inch long. It was a staple for all our kids as they developed their teeth. They are great to hold, fiddle, or gnaw. They can be attached to your stroller, car seat, or backpack using the links above. You can also put them in the freezer to cool them off if your child is having a particularly hard time with teething.

Keys

Whether purchased by their parents or as a gift, a set of plastic keys is a classic toy that ends up in every child's toy box or diaper bag. These two to three inch colored plastic keys on a ring have different textures, sometimes make noise, are good to grab, and are easy to clip to the end of a chain. Babies love the textures and, apparently, the taste.

Stars and Rings

The particular version of this toy we purchased was a stack of four different colored plastic stars stacked on a six-inch tall dowel on a circular base. The stars get smaller as you go up the stack. Each time your child places a star on the stack she is rewarded by the toy making a noise. When the last star is placed on the stack they all light up and the toy plays a little tune. Sidney just loved it. An alternative to the stars is a stack of different colored rings.

Whack-a-Ball

Sandy says this was one of her favorite toys as a little girl which explains her fascination with the arcade game "Whack-a-mole". So it didn't surprise us when all our kids loved it. The front of this twelve-inch tall toy is made of clear plastic. Inside there are three switchbacks with assorted wheels and gears. Four colored balls fit neatly into color-matched holes at the top. Children learn to associate the colors. Then, when they whack the ball with the supplied spring loaded hammer, they watch them work there way down to the trough at the bottom. Calvin loved it so much we had to buy a new hammer.

Metal Xylophone

There's something about banging and noise that is fascinating to kids, or at least our kids. One way to cultivate that is with a tiny xylophone. Ours was about sixteen inches long with eight colored, metal keys. It came with a drum stick with an oversized end. Each key made a different noise. The reward of hearing the noises made by the keys was an enticement for them to build hand-eye coordination. An alternative to this is a mini upright piano. Baby can bang on the keys and get rewarded by a variety of sounds. The ones made by Melissa and Doug (www.melissaanddoug.com) were a particular favorite. Actually, just about anything made by Melissa and Doug was popular in our house.

Drums

Sidney liked whacking things so much we bought her a drum. While on vacation, we found a musical instrument store in a charming little town where I jokingly asked the proprietor if he had a set of small bongos. He showed me a beautiful set of drums that cost about three hundred dollars. I thanked him and said that was a little more than I wanted to spend on a fifteen month old. He smiled and produced a set of colorful toy bongos made by Latin Percussions. For those of you who don't know, as I didn't, Latin Percussions makes some serious professional equipment. As it happens, they also make kid's versions of some of it. The drum we got cost less than forty dollars (in 2003) and Sidney banged on the drum all day. Check out the complete line of musical instruments for children at www.lprhythmix.com.

Chapter Fourteen - Books, Books, and More Books

When a friend of mine described the shelves and shelves of children's books he had, I thought he was exaggerating. But after about two years of parenthood, guess what, we had bookcases filled with them. Just like with toys, books can be very age targeted. I think they also multiply at night.

It is incredibly important to read to your children because it stimulates their minds. (There's more about this in the *Talk to your Baby* section of **Parenting Tips – Stuff about Baby**.) When our kids were little, Sandy would read whatever was nearby when she nursed. As they got older we made reading stories part of the nighttime, going to bed ritual. There are some books that seem to be a staple because they're the ones we were given multiple copies of.

When we first started reading children's books to Sidney, she inevitably wanted to hold the book. That's why books for toddlers are usually made of thick paper or cardboard. We called these "board" books. Indeed, some of our favorites, that we read every night had to be replaced so Ellie, and Calvin after her, could enjoy (and destroy) them. So library books are probably out. Board books are usually quite short and simple. They are perfect to for associating letters, numbers, and objects with pictures so your baby can learn these things by association. Examples of these are:

> ***Baby's First Words*** (there are several of these by different authors)
>
> ***The Number Board Book***, by DK Publishing
>
> Just about anything by Boynton.

The "Staples"

It is clearly not my intent to list every book that could end up in your library. Before Sidney was born our book library took up about twelve inches of shelf space. Now it takes up three bookcases. But our library started out with a few books I refer to as the staples. Don't be surprised if you get multiple copies of these.

> ***Goodnight Moon***, by Margaret Wise Brown
>
> ***Pat the Bunny***, by Dorothy Kunhardt
>
> ***The Runaway Bunny***, by Margaret Wise Brown
>
> ***Where the Wild Things Are***, by Maurice Sendak
>
> Anything by Dr. Seuss and also The Boynton Books

Others We Really Liked

Make Way for Ducklings, by Robert McCloskey

The Way I Feel (also known as the Upside-down Book), by Janan Cain

Close Your Eyes (Little Tiger), by Kate Banks

If Kisses Were Colors, by Janet Lawler (one of my personal favorites)

I'm Gonna Like Me, by Jamie Lee Curtis

Yesterday I Had the Blues, by Jeron Ashford Frame

Chapter Fifteen - Stuff for Keeping Clean

This section outlines the different gear you'll need to keep yourself and your baby clean. Keeping your baby clean can be roughly divided into day and night. The daytime challenge will consist of keeping her hands and face relatively free of debris, but by far the most common, time-consuming activity will be diaper changing. Once she's sleeping well and you can leave nighttime diaper changes behind, the primary nighttime task will be the tubby before bed.

Cleaning the Umbilical Cord

When you came home from the hospital, you didn't have that nice little belly button that you have now. No, you had a two- to three-inch long navy blue appendage. Ick! That's the technical term for what it looked like because after they cut the cord and take the clamp off, they put a drying solution on it that has the added effect of turning the cord navy blue.

While the cord is attached to your baby you have to make sure the base, where it's attached to the body, is clean and dry so it doesn't get infected. Our hospital recommended that we use alcohol to clean the base of the cord daily, but there's research that says to do nothing and let nature take its course. Ask your doctor, as it's a big deal if it gets infected. If you do clean the cord with alcohol be prepared for a little fussing, but once the cord comes off, it's bubbles away!

Baby Oil and Cradle Cap

Ever wonder why they call it baby oil? Right, it's for babies. Even wonder what you use it for? Well I'm sure there are many other uses, but we were taught to use it to treat cradle cap. Until we had a baby I didn't know what that was either. Basically it's really dry skin on the scalp. To treat it, you rub in some baby oil. Brush it in gently with the extra soft genuine plastic baby brush they give you at the hospital. Then shampoo with baby shampoo. His hair will be a little greasy the next day, and it may take a couple of treatments, but this treatment will generally take care of the dry skin.

Burp Cloths

Burp cloths are simply old-fashioned 100% cotton cloth diapers. To get them extra soft, wash and dry them, with fabric softener, between twenty to one hundred times. I'm not exaggerating. Get them as early as you can once you know you're having a baby and every time you're doing a load of whites run them through the wash.

I'll let you in on a little secret. You can always pick out the parents with young babies because there are little patches of crusty stuff on their shoulders. At the office one day I realized I must have been holding one of the kids the last time I wore the blazer I had on because it had a crusty patch on the shoulder. It only takes a second for a child to wipe her mouth on your shoulder. So look around and see how many parents you can pick out of a crowd. And it doesn't end with infants. If your child is crying, you're going to pick him up. And then a few hours later you'll scratch the crust off your shoulder. An excellent way to avoid crusty shoulders is to put a burp cloth on your shoulder before you pick up your baby. I could never seem to take that extra step even though it is especially helpful if you are wearing nice clothes

Burp cloths have many uses besides protecting your shoulder. For example, they're good for putting on the changing table when you have a particularly big load to change. Then you can just throw them in the laundry and you don't have to change the pad cover, which can be a little difficult to do with only one hand. Sandy put a burp cloth over her arm when she breastfed so Baby's head rested on the cloth, not her skin. This was much more comfortable, and cut down on heat and sweat.

Bottom Cleaning

Having a baby means changing diapers; there's no getting around it. Changing diapers means you have to do a little bottom cleaning. (Pun intended.) Baby's bottom is extremely sensitive so the type of wipe and method of wiping are very important. Even the softest of paper towels may feel like sandpaper to your baby, so you need to use something made especially for babies. What's more, if there's too much moisture left on her bottom when you put the diaper on, she could develop a rash. When that happens, you'll want a good diaper cream.

Cotton Wipes and Bottle Warmers

It stands to reason that most people go straight to the store-bought prepackaged wipes when they have a baby. We would have too except both the "how to keep your baby alive" instructor at the hospital and our pediatrician said to use cotton pads and water for the first several months. The reason for this, as noted above, is that a newborn's bottom is extremely

Jed Gibson

sensitive and wipes, even "natural" ones, have chemicals in them that can cause irritation.

For the first several months of your baby's life there's not a lot to clean up. Believe it or not, urine is sterile, so not much cleaning is necessary. The first output your baby will have is a tar-like substance called merconium. Once he gets through this his "output" (if you're breastfeeding) is about a tablespoon of stuff the consistency of Dijon mustard.

I know using cotton pads and water sounds inconvenient, but it's really not. I found that using a bottle warmer made by Advent was a simple way to keep warm water on hand for changes at home. A bottle warmer looks a lot like an oversized insulated mug without a handle. It's got an adjustable heating element that keeps the water warm. The reservoir accepts a bottle or jar, usually of the same brand as the warmer. I played with the water level in the warmer reservoir and once it was just right, marked the level with a Sharpie. That way I'd always know how much water to put in the reservoir so it wouldn't overflow when I inserted the jar. Fill a feeding bottle or jar with

142

the appropriate amount of water and adjust the temp on the warmer to the lowest setting. Then go to CVS and get lots of cotton face cleaning pads. Don't worry if you get too many, they won't spoil. To clean your baby's bottom, simply dip a cotton pad in the water, squeeze out the excess, and wipe. Make sure to change the water in the jar every day and clean the reservoir regularly.

Prepackaged Wipes

We were pretty good about using cotton pads and water for the first several months of our kids' lives, but that's not always convenient if, for instance, you're out of the house. So you'll need some wipes to travel with. There are several brands, like Huggies, that make a travel-size package, which fits into your diaper bag. For refills, we bought the wipes in bulk. By bulk I mean wholesale club–type cartons the size of a small microwave that had four "bricks" of wipes. The plastic bags the "bricks" came in were resealable to keep the wipes moist. You can peel off a stack and use them to refill your wipe warmer and your travel pack.

Wipe Warmer

Ever sit down on a toilet seat that's ice cold? Fun, huh? Well that's probably how it feels to your baby if you're using room temperature, meaning cold, wipes. Get yourself a wipe warmer or several if you have multiple changing stations. Wipe warmers are plug-in warming boxes about three inches tall and eight inches long that you can fill with prepackaged wipes from the "brick" you got at the wholesale club. If you use the warmer infrequently, don't be surprised if the wipes on the bottom become completely dried out. You can add a little water in a pinch, or simply change them out for fresh ones when this happens.

You will start your baby on solid foods between four and six months of age, depending on what your doctor recommends. When you do this their solid output starts to get bigger and smellier. Little cotton pads will no longer do the trick and you'll need something larger. You'll also start to look forward to the day you no longer have to change diapers. Okay, you start looking forward to that the day you come home from the hospital.

As an aside, one of the things we read was not to refer to the smell when changing diapers. Once your baby can understand what you are saying he'll remember this and may think that poop is bad and therefore could have trouble getting potty trained. So we learned that instead of saying, "Yuck, smelly poopies," to say, "Wow, big poopies."

Diaper Cream

Before I had children I often wondered what diaper cream was. It's is generally not for chafing as I thought, but to coat your baby's bottom so it can heal from a rash. Rashes on a baby's bottom can come from a variety of things. For example, during the course of adjusting to life your baby will eat many new things. Not all of which will agree with her. There will be the inevitable bout of the D word, diarrhea. Or there may simply be too much moisture if her diaper is wet for too long.

We used two different types of cream: the thick white stuff that's zinc based, and medicated cream that's kind of yellowish. Both had the consistency of paste. You doctor can tell you when to use which. It's a good idea to have some in your diaper bag as well as near your changing table(s).

The Size Mystery, Again

The size mystery applies to diapers, just as it does to baby clothing. (See *The Size Mystery* in **Clothing – Stuff to Wear**.) However, in the case of diapers you'll find the information you need on the side of the box as opposed to the tag, like with clothes. We found it most helpful to ignore the age designation and chose our diaper size based on height and/or weight. Once you've selected a size that works, it should be good for a while. Then the next time you're shopping you can simply purchase them by the size on the box, for example, 2T. You'll eventually have to change sizes, but the frequency of that will depend on how fast your baby grows. Just be careful not to get diapers that are too large or you run the risk of leakage and/or chafing.

Diapers

The diaper wars rage on. The two main players when we had our kids were Pampers and Huggies. In my opinion, Huggies tended to be a little more cutting edge, with things like "triple-sealed elastic seams to keep moisture in." There are also several "generic" brands. A friend of ours used generic and was very happy with them. We tried just about everything including some "natural" diapers. We found that the natural ones weighed about ten pounds dry and were good for one "pee" before they fell apart. One thing we never tried were cloth diapers because, well, yuck! In the end we used kind of a hodgepodge of brands and types, settling on Pampers for daily use and Huggies for overnight.

When our babies were small, we started with Pampers Swaddlers. Of course, all babies are small but they make a special type just for newborns that have a semicircular cutout that goes around the umbilical cord. This prevents irritation. Once the cord came off we switched to regular Swaddlers and used them for sizes one and two.

We felt that the Huggies product was softer but needed more padding to be as absorbent as Pampers. So during the day we used Pampers "Dry Baby." However, after the kids got to about eighteen pounds and were sleeping through the night (hooray), their nightly output started to get through their diapers. For this we used a product made by Huggies called "Overnights." They start at size four, had lots of extra padding and kept the kids dry. We felt they were a little bulky for daytime use.

Diaper Pail

So you've just changed a diaper. You've got this warm smelly bundle of poop in your hand. What do you do with it? Being anal [pun intended], I rolled it into a tight little sausage using the Velcro straps from the diaper to hold it together. I found it easier to manage and control the odors this way. But I still had this diaper to deal with. If you love nasty smells, you can just throw that puppy into the garbage can. The house will smell so bad in no time that the cat will leave. (Even my wife, who hated the cat, didn't do this.)

There are several brands of "diaper pails" out there. There's one call "Diaper Champ" that lets you use regular garbage bags. You push the diaper into a cylinder with a kind of airlock and lift a lever to drop it into the pail. I believe the most popular is the "Diaper Genie." This requires a special "bag" that you insert. Each time you put in a diaper, you twist the "bag" and it seals the diaper and the smell into what we affectionately called the "sausage." The newer ones have a wide mouth and a built-in bag cutter. You can get the refills in bulk at your local warehouse-type store (BJs, Sam's Club, etc.). We tried both "Champ" and "Genie" and ultimately settled on the Diaper Genie.

Tubs and Tubby Time

There are a variety of tubs for cleaning infants you can purchase for tubby time. Ours was padded and had a built-in thermometer. Some have slings that suspend the baby in/over the water. There are also travel tubs that are inflatable. The key we looked for was that it would be comfortable for a little body and had a built-in sloping backrest so we wouldn't worry about her sliding into the water. Of course, you also have the option of getting in the tub (the regular tub) with your baby. I felt this was inappropriate when the girls got to be about a year old, but personal opinion will vary.

Bathing an infant is a unique experience. They're so small and delicate, yet they can be so strong. Then you get them wet and soapy and they're real slippery. First off, make sure the water's not too hot. Remember, you've been using your fingers for twenty to forty years, so they're not as sensitive as your baby's skin. Test the water with your forearm. Although our tub had a little built-in thermometer, we still used our arm as a barometer (actually, thermometer). Better safe than sorry.

The general advice we got in our "how not to kill your baby" class at the hospital was to start from the bottom and work our way up to the head. It may be counter-intuitive but you don't want to wet the head or hair until the end. Cover him with a towel as you go to keep him warm and wash his hair last, as he'll lose the most heat through his head. When you clean his eyelids, use a separate, clean cotton-ball for each eye to ensure you don't transmit any bacteria from one eye to the other. All the water you use for cleaning should come from the tap or a separate bowl, not the tub. You don't want to be wiping your baby with dirty bath water. Lastly, you shouldn't give your baby anything but a sponge bath until the cord falls off. See *Cleaning the Umbilical Cord* above.

Baby Washcloths

Washcloths for babies are smaller, softer versions of the washcloths grownups use. You can get them in any baby supply store. You might think you could just use a regular household washcloth. The Neanderthal in me wondered why I couldn't use something from the rag pile, or paper towels. But my wife kindly pointed out that babies have very soft, sensitive skin and therefore we needed to have soft baby washcloths. In addition to use for cleaning, you can lay a warm wet one over your baby's tummy to keep him warm in the tub.

Baby Towels

This goes along the same line as washcloths above: they're soft. They're also smaller than grownup bath towels, so they're easier to handle. In addition, many of them have a pocket in the corner that serves as a hood you can put over your baby's head when you take him out of the tub. It'll dry whatever hair he has, and keep him warm. When your baby gets to be about twenty pounds, or thirty inches, or a year old (that size mystery again), you may want to consider switching to grownup towels.

Chapter Sixteen - Safety Gear – AKA "Baby-proofing"

When we first got pregnant we went around frantically getting the house ready and "safe." Our whole perspective on safety changed once we had a child. For example, I had just installed (meaning placed) speakers on a low wall in the living room only to realize that we would constantly be worried about our child pulling on the wire and bringing the speakers down on her head. Everything in the house had to be evaluated from the point of view of a curious child. If it could be pulled down or swallowed or she could get cut on or tangled in something, it needed to be locked down or put away. We lived in an old house when we had our babies. Depending on your living arrangements you may have some different issues. For example, newer houses may come with tamper-proof outlets already installed.

Outlet Covers

Starting in 2009 many new houses were required to be built using tamper-proof (read kid-proof) outlets. These have built-in child protection so you can't jam things into them.

Sometimes they're also grownup proof, as quite often I couldn't plug things into them in our new house.

For our older house we child-proofed the outlets so our curious kids wouldn't experiment with them. We found two different kinds of devices that served this purpose. The basic ones are plastic inserts that you plug into your outlets and render them inert. We had these in a couple of places, but it is possible for your toddler to take them out. Indeed, a friend of mine told me that shortly after his daughter turned two she came and handed him a pile of them after she took them all out of the wall.

The other option is to replace the outlet cover with one that has spring loaded individual rotating cover pieces for each plug. Plugging something in requires that you partially insert the plug, twist a quarter turn, and then push. When you pull out the plug, the cover snaps back covering the power source. This way the outlet is easy to use and immediately off line when you unplug something. To me, these were much better, although more expensive. The only drawback we found was that the big plugs, like the kind with power transformers on the end, won't stay in because of the extra distance from the outlet to the face of the cover. The brand we used was Safety First.

Cabinet and Drawer Latches

Some friends came over for dinner one night and started laughing hysterically at the sight of a fourteen-month-old Sidney pulling everything out of one of our kitchen drawers. Indeed, this is quite common for a child that age. They were laughing because they went through the same thing with their daughter. We made sure the drawer in question was baby friendly because we wanted Sidney to be able to explore. However, many (actually most) drawers and cabinets are not places you want your child to have access. Cabinet and drawer latches are a must. It doesn't matter the brand as long as they work every time. We chose to get ones that not only stopped the drawer or door from opening, but they also stopped them from closing too, so tiny fingers wouldn't get pinched. You also need to be ready for the grunts and groans you and your guests will make when you try to open a drawer that's got a latch.

Swinging Door Stops

Yes, most doors swing, unless they are sliding doors. What I am referring to here are the old-fashioned swinging doors that can open both into and out of a room. They tend to be spring loaded so they will stop in the closed position. You know, like in a restaurant kitchen. Not many houses have swinging doors anymore, but if yours does I strongly recommend you get a swinging door stop. These are U- shaped foam bumpers that fit onto the side or top of the door. They prevent the door from closing on little fingers. Once Sidney got mobile, she took great pleasure in pushing the door closed, especially in the dog's face. It was nice to know that no one would get hurt.

Gates

What's scarier, the thought of your baby crawling up to the precipice at the top of the stairs or hearing a high-pitch giggle and realizing your toddler just climbed the stairs to the second floor, alone, and is staring down at you from ten feet above your head? In neither case does your baby perceive the danger. Both make your heart stop. So, save that heart stopping for a romantic evening with your wife (there's more about babysitters in **Commentary on Life - Stuff about You**) and get yourself some good gates and put them at the top **and** bottom of each set of stairs. Point made?

There are two factors to consider when choosing a gate: material and means of attachment. Generally, gates are made

Jed Gibson

of either plastic or wood, but occasionally metal, and they're either permanently or temporarily attached. Material choice is purely personal or one of convenience, based on what's available. Permanent gates are attached to the wall by means of screwed-in hardware and will probably be there until your youngest child is three to five years old. They have a basic hinge and clasp that lets you lock them in place when they're closed and swing them out of the way when they're open. Temporary gates are usually pressure attached by means of some sort of lever you raise or lower that expands them into place. It's always good to have one of these around to take on trips. Being safety freaks, we shied away from press fit for everyday use because there's nothing like permanent attachment to ensure stability. We also found that to truly get a solid fit that won't budge with a press fit gate, you're taking the paint off the wall a little at a time. So we settled on permanently attached wooden gates at the top and bottom of both stairs.

Window Guards

Take a look at the screens on your windows. If they're relatively new, they have a little warning label that says they won't stop a child from falling out the window. Don't take that lightly. Even a fall from the first-floor window can be bad. If you want to ensure that your windows are safe, you can install window guards. There are a variety of types, including metal bars, mesh, and little locks you can put on double-hung windows to restrict how far they open. Be careful with window locks because bedroom windows also serve as a way out of the house if there's a fire. The metal bar type can expand to the width, or height, of your window and snaps into a receiver you attach to the window frame. The bars are close together so your child can't fit his head through them. I slept really well knowing that when, not if, Sidney or Ellie or Calvin climbed up on the window sill, they weren't going anywhere.

Incidentally, fall protection became part of many building codes starting in 2006. Window guards were only required if the window sills are closer than twenty-four inches to the floor inside if the ground outside is more than six-feet down. I tried that argument on Sandy, but she still wanted window guards.

Toilet Seat Locks

At the risk of getting too graphic, consider falling head first into a pool of water half as deep as you are tall without the arm strength or coordination to get out. Like window guards and gates, this is another topic that you really don't want to dwell on the ramifications of not spending a couple of bucks to ensure safety. Kids, toddlers are curious. They love to play. Set down a bowl of water and see how long it takes for a baby who can crawl to start playing in it. Why would you set down a bowl of water? Got a dog or cat?

Toilet locks are simple to install if you know how to use a screwdriver. The ones we used were arms that swing over the seat locking it down and making it impossible to play in the toilet bowl. It had a button that needed to be pressed in order to open it. All of the ones we installed were broken by a guest who couldn't read the "press" label on the button. They would still swing, but they no longer locked. Another issue I learned the hard way was how difficult they were to open with one hand while holding a baby. That said I wouldn't have removed them for the world.

Nontoxic Cleaners

Did I mention that my wife is a tad overprotective? When we had Sidney, she threw out all the regular household cleaners and bought all-natural, non-toxic cleaners. I thought this was a bit much, but no harm done. Then I read an article that linked childhood asthma to the chemicals in many household cleaners. Your basic second-hand fumes theory. So now she's not looking like such a freak. And yes, I told her, and put up with the gloating (it was brief).

Chapter Seventeen - Medicine and First Aid

We had so much to learn about caring for a baby when we had our first that we attended several safety classes. Even with all our research, we were completely unprepared the first time Sidney got sick. There is a wide array of first aid gadgetry that you'll want to stock. We also had to learn a whole new list of medicines and remedies and then we had to understand the nuances of dosage for babies and toddlers versus grownups.

Thermometers

There is no getting around the fact that at some point your child is going to get a fever. When that happens, you'll need to take his temperature in order to know what action to take. Your basic choices are under the tongue and in the ear. We were told that rectal thermometers can be dangerous for infants, not to mention a pain in the – okay, a pain to use. We had both types and ultimately used the ear thermometer exclusively. Ear thermometers are battery powered and have a sleeve on the end that fits into, you guessed it, your ear. Many doctors' offices use them now instead of the under-the-tongue type. I remember reading an article about children's thermometers where the author thought it was ridiculous that anyone would spend the money on an ear thermometer when you could get an oral thermometer for one quarter the price. I question whether the author had children. What I do know is that the ear thermometer is not only quite reliable and gives us a temperature reading in about five seconds, it is also incredibly easy to use. And as a special bonus you can use it on yourself.

Snot Sucker

Newborns can't blow their noses. In fact, ours were just getting the hang of it at three years old. Just about the only reflex a newborn has is to sneeze. When that happens, usually you'll need a tissue. Since a newborn drinks all her meals, when her nose is stuffed it is really difficult to eat. (You try drinking through a straw with a stuffed up nose.)

I have to admit, "snot sucker" is my wife's term, but it is an apt name for the bulb syringe. Because when the nose is stuffed, that's how you clean it out. They will probably give you a cheap one at the hospital after your baby is born. You get about one use out of it because it's impossible to clean. If you're planning on using one, get a good one that has a removable stopper at the end. This will allow you to open and clean it. Someone has also come up with the idea of using a tube you can literally suck the snot out of you baby's nose. It sounds gross, but it may be effective and easy. The brand I saw was named, "Snot Sucker." Go figure. There is also a saline solution that you can get to spray up your baby's nose to loosen things up before using the "sucker." There is, of course, research that says that these really don't do any good. That the nose just fills up with snot again. This may be true. I know when I'm stuffed, my nose keeps filling up. But if your baby can breathe through her nose for a few minutes you may be able to get in a feeding. Regardless, it's a good idea to get your doctor's opinion about both the "sucker" and the saline.

First Aid Kit

When I think "first aid kit," I think of Band-Aids and ointment. The ones we found for babies were more like tool kits. Before Sidney was born we bought a really cool all-in-one first aid kit made by Safety First. It had nail clippers, a thermometer, tweezers, and a medicine measuring syringe. The only thing we used were the clippers, and as you'll note below, we went out and got several more. We never had occasion to use the tweezers. We got a high-tech thermometer, and the medicine syringe was too big to fit into any of the medicine bottles we used. A nice thought, but if I had it to do over again I'd just buy the individual pieces: clipper, thermometer, and syringe.

Fingernail Clippers

Baby's fingernails are like razor blades. Ellie had (and has) this amazing grip. She could grab a hunk of what you thought was very taut flesh and make it into a handle. That's painful enough, but add the occasional fingernail and it's excruciating. To be clear, long fingernails on an infant are about a thirty-second of an inch long. They grow to that length, from fully clipped, in about five days. The other danger of your baby having "long" nails is that she can easily scratch and cut herself, so you'll need a way to shorten those little razors. Get yourself about five pair of good **infant** fingernail clippers. Why five? They're so small you'll lose them the minute you put them down. Don't, under any circumstances, try to use adult nail clippers. They're too big and you could really hurt your baby.

Note: when your baby is born her nails are kind of attached to the end of her fingers. You can't use a clipper at all. For the first few weeks you'll need to gently use a nail file. Once the nails start growing out past the end of the finger you can switch to a clipper.

Medicine Syringe

Medicine syringes look like hypodermic needles but the end is larger. You use them to squirt medicine into your baby's mouth. Every bottle of Infant Advil we bought came with its own little medicine syringe. Save them because they're real lifesavers for other medicines as well. These little throw-aways are good up to about 1.875 ml. Once you get over that dosage, you'll obviously need a larger syringe. Many pharmacies will give syringes to you when you fill a prescription for a liquid. Get a couple. You won't want to go searching for them in the middle of the night when your baby's screaming and you're exhausted. Just keep in mind, if the tube is too wide, you'll have trouble getting it into the medicine bottle, and with the baby screaming and you being exhausted you may come up with some interesting work-arounds. We took to pouring the medicine into a Dixie cup and then sucking it into the syringe. This is particularly helpful when the bottle is running low.

<u>Humidifier</u>

It seems like every doctor we talked to told us it's a good idea to have a humidifier in our baby's room. They said the moist air does them good and the white noise is soothing. You can find other ways to producing white noise in the *Music and White Noise* section of **Parenting Tips – Stuff about Baby**. If you do want to use a humidifier you need to be warned about, and possibly overcome, the latest four-letter word: mold.

As an architect I've done a lot of research about mold remediation. I took a class given by an expert instructor who said that cold mist humidifiers are bad. There are a lot of myths about what causes mold to grow. One is that humidity, or moist air, causes it. That's not exactly true. Mold needs three things to grow: the right temperature, which is just about always the case inside your house. Food, for example the soft organic paper like you find on drywall. Lastly, it needs moisture, which can come from a leak, condensation, or spraying cold mist on the wall. I have to admit, it's a dilemma with no easy answer. So beware.

Our doctor told us to use a cold-mist humidifier for the girls. These are so safe mechanically that we were comfortable putting it on the floor of Sidney's room. She pulled it apart once a week, but there was nothing she could hurt herself on (except, of course, the electrical cord.) If you get one with a wick, make sure to change it regularly because they tend to grow stuff.

We ultimately got a hot-mist humidifier. It heated the water to boiling, killing most bacteria, and then ran it through an ultraviolet light to kill anything that's left. This safely put moisture into the air in the nursery. The drawback was that the internal parts got hot, so we made sure it was installed in a way it couldn't be reached by a curious child. Once we renovated our old house we put in a whole house humidifier. But you have to be careful with those too because if not installed, used, or maintained properly, they could cause mold to grow in your home for the reasons outlined previously.

Baby Monitors

If you really want to go overboard with these you can get them with cameras. Most parents, ourselves included, think that's a bit much. There's some great research in *Consumer Reports* on which ones are best, but some of the best insight can come from the experts, meaning other parents. Being a technophile, I immediately went for the high-tech, bells and whistles monitors made by reputable high-tech gadget makers like V-

Tech, or Uniden. Fortunately we were overheard by a helpful parent who said something like, "Yeah we tried that one too and it was really awful, the Safety 1st works best." We ended up with a two-channel monitor with one base and two receivers. The base went in the baby's room. The receiver you can carry around. If you're planning on having more that one child, two channels can be quite handy because you may want to have bases in two places like the nursery and the two-year-old's room. With two channels we could simply switch the receiver from one channel to the other to hear what was going on in either location.

The technology for baby monitors, like so many other baby products is constantly evolving. I'm sure they have Bluetooth monitors that connect to your iPhone or ones that slide under the mattress and sound an alarm if your baby stops breathing now, but they didn't exist when Sidney was born. So, do some research in *Consumer Reports* and/or speak to other parents before you buy.

Medications

We were totally unprepared the first time Sidney got a cold. I guess we thought we'd see it coming. We didn't. She was five months old and woke up inconsolable at 2:00 am. We went through our normal litany of things to calm a crying baby, but it became clear by 2:30 that this was not normal crankiness. Fortunately, we had a fantastic pediatrician whom we called and woke up. He was a little groggy, but he identified that it was just a cold and said to give Sidney some Pediacare. Unfortunately, we didn't have any of that. Nor did we have the Triaminic or Benadryl he asked about. He ultimately talked us through giving her some over-the-counter adult medicine, which he adeptly dose adjusted for an infant. I don't think I will ever forget the look on Sidney's face when she got her first taste of NyQuil. With all due respect to Vicks, that's some nasty-tasting stuff. But the medicine worked wonders; Sidney went back to sleep, and the next day we did a little shopping.

A caution about dosage: Several doctors have pointed out that the younger the intended patient, the more concentrated the medicine. Don't ask why. Some wise pharmaceutical genius made the decision eons ago, and so it remains. So be careful. What this means is that Infant Advil is much more concentrated than Children's, which is more concentrated than Adults'. Another slightly irritating medication mystery is that many medicines don't provide infant dosage; they simply say "two and under, consult your doctor." Dosage is based on many things, including weight and the maturity of the digestive track. After two years old, I'm told the averages flatten out a bit. But under two, you should call your doctor.

As with toys and gadgets, the science behind the medicine is constantly changing. At one point a few years ago all toddler cough syrup was removed from the shelves. This was particularly shocking because this stuff had been used for thirty years. So check with your doctor and look at online medical sites like www.askdrsears.com or www.webmd.com.

The Short List

Below is a suggested list of what you might want to have around the house. I would strongly recommend that you speak to your pediatrician **before** you have your baby and create an up-to-date list. You still may have to call at 2:00 am for dosage, but at least you'll be prepared. Once you get some parenting experience under your belt, you'll start to see the warning signs, which always seem to be on a Friday after the doctor's office closes. But at least you can get someone on the phone at a decent hour. Another suggestion is to get a list of dosages each time you see your doctor and keep it on your fridge.

<u>Antihistamine</u> – Our doctor preferred Benadryl. Another choice is Triaminic. Because both come only in children's strength, you'll need to get the appropriate dosage for an infant from your doctor.

<u>Antihistamine with decongestant</u> - Also known as Benadryl Plus or Triaminic Allergy. Our doctor usually recommended Triaminic. Pediacare also makes a product for this and, unlike the others, it comes in infant dosage.

<u>Cold remedies</u> – Benadryl and Triaminic both make a version of these. They are labeled as, "Cough and Cold" or "Cold and Flu." They contain the same ingredients that are in the "allergy" medicine (antihistamine with decongestant) with an added cough suppressant.

<u>Ipecac</u> – We have been fortunate enough to never have to use this. **Our pediatrician told us to get it and never use it unless we were specifically instructed to**

do so by him. As I understand it, this is a compound that will cause your child to empty his stomach (throw up) of everything in it. This is very important if he swallows something bad. Keep it around in safe place and hope you never use it.

<u>Mylacon</u> – This is the most amazing drug ever invented. It breaks up gas bubbles. You may not think that's a big deal, but when your baby is screaming with gas pain, you'll understand. We kept it around in many places. Check with your doctor as to what age it's safe to use.

<u>Pain Relief</u> –This is your basic pain medication, also known as an analgesic. For the first three to six months of our baby's lives we were told to use infant Tylenol. It's apparently gentler on the stomach than Advil. After Sidney was old enough our doctor switched us over to infant Advil. He said it acts faster. Anything that gets your child out of pain faster is a good thing. One bottle of infant strength was only good for about four doses.

<u>Pedialyte</u> – Ever try this stuff? Yuck! It tastes nasty but it serves an important role. If, meaning when, your baby gets diarrhea you need to replace the electrolytes in his body. We learned, the hard way, that once you open the bottle it's only good for about forty-eight hours. So get a few small bottles and throw them in the back of your fridge for that fateful day. Our kids preferred orange but your doctor may want you to only use clear.

Section 3 – Lessons

Aside from all the physical "stuff" you need to care for a baby, there are a lot of lessons you pick up along the way. Some of it is common sense, but some of it I wish someone had told me. This includes advice on not taking advice. Your baby will consume your life, take all your time, energy, and a good bit of your money. You'll love it, most of the time. But there will be times when you're tired and need a break. An important part of raising a child is making sure you take time for yourself and your partner. If you're happy there's a much greater chance your baby will be happy.

Chapter Eighteen - Parenting Tips – Stuff about Baby

We have three happy, creative, loving children. While I like to think it's simply from good genes, the fact is a lot of it is coached. Hopefully, that coaching will serve them well and they can pass it along to their children. In addition to various interpersonal skills we learned, there are also a few tidbits we stumbled upon you might find helpful in the sections below.

Take Those Pictures Early, Your Baby Will Get Acne

A little known fact that no one told us is that babies get serious acne. It has something to do with the hormone balancing and the adjustment to not floating they go through shortly after birth. At about three weeks of age they'll get kind of bumpy. Not to worry, it's normal. The reason I mention this is you will most likely be sending birth announcements. Everyone will want to see a picture of the new addition. Take the pictures early (yes, I know you'll be exhausted and disheveled) or wait until the acne clears up.

The Advice Everyone Gives

Everyone, I mean everyone, is going to give you parenting advice. It gets to be a bit much. My advice? Smile and say thank you, and do what you think is best. It can be trying at times. You don't really want to tell your mother to piss off. Okay, well maybe you do, but it's best that you don't. This is not to say there's anything wrong with the advice you're getting, or that there's anything wrong with seeking advice. It's that you won't agree with everything you hear, and while everyone has good intentions, it's your child.

Parenting Is Guessing

I have come to believe that a lot of parenting is guessing. I was with a friend of mine when her three-year-old fell down. It looked pretty bad, but as a mother she knew it really wasn't. She looked at him and said, "Brush it off Tim." He got up, brushed his arm off, and went about his playing. I was amazed. When I asked her how she knew it would work she simply told me, "Sometimes you just get lucky." I had no kids at the time but I learned an important parenting tip that day. Sometimes you just have to guess. I won't lay odds on how often it works. But it does work.

Another example is a phone conversation I was having with Sandy where I could hear Sidney playing in the background. Suddenly Sandy wasn't talking to me, but to Sidney, who had obviously gotten into something she shouldn't have. "Put it down! No don't touch it. No don't touch it. No don't touch it. No. No. No. Mommy said no." She wasn't yelling, just persistent. Finally, Sidney got the message, stopped trying to touch "it," and started to whine and cry. But Sandy told her "Mommy's not going to listen to you whine right now, you can do it later." Through the phone I heard a tiny, but happy, "Okay," and Sidney went off to play. Wow!

Don't Freak Out When They Fall Down

When your toddler falls down, and this will be a frequent thing, she may look to you on how to react. If she's truly hurt, comfort her. However, if it's a minor fall, try not to freak out, since not every little scrape or fall is a major crisis. If you remain calm she may just brush it off and keep on playing (see above). What you're going for here is self-reliance and teaching how to deal with minor issues herself. Usually when Sidney had a minor fall and was upset I reassured her and told her I knew how scary it can be to fall down. You will also learn to identify the major, or hurtful, falls. For me the tell-tale sign was silence. If Sidney opened her mouth and nothing came out as she slowly sucked in her breath, the longer the silence, the louder the scream that followed. When this happened I would speak to her in a soothing tone telling her I know it hurt, I know it was scary, and that she'd be alright.

The Crying Game

Ever buy a new set of speakers for your home? When you listen to them in the store, they all sound the same. But if you take the time to sit down and listen to your favorite music on one pair at a time they suddenly are not the same. The sound of a baby crying is much the same. Before we had Sidney I couldn't tell one baby crying from another. After she was born, a strange thing happened. I was sitting at a child's birthday party and one of the kids started to cry. I momentarily cocked my head to listen. "Nope, not Sidney," I thought. I was amazed. I thought it was some kind of magic or myth that people could recognize their baby simply by her cry, but after I became a parent it was second nature.

There is another level to this that you soon learn. Your baby has more than one cry. Remember, there are only a few ways an infant can communicate. Laughter, of course, is the most glorious. But for most other things there are a variety of grunts and cries. You will learn to distinguish between hunger, pain, exhaustion, boredom, and frustration. All it takes is a little focus and love.

Sleeping Through the Night and Trust

Right after you have your baby everyone will ask you some version of the same thing. "Getting any sleep?" "How's the baby sleeping?" "She sleeping through the night yet?" You may take this opportunity to mess with people and say, "Why, yes, she's sleeping fourteen hours a night. Has been since her second week." All parents will be grossly jealous of this. Of course, the chances of that actually happening are slim to none, but in your haze you've got to have some fun.

Babies don't sleep. That is to say, they generally don't sleep for very long at one time. We were under the impression when we had Sidney that babies sleep seventeen hours a day. Sandy was so confident of this fact that she planned on refinishing the screened porch. Since fate loves temptation, Sidney was not one to nap. At all. Ever. For the first several weeks, if not months, you can expect your baby to wake up every two hours, doesn't matter whether its night or day. They also have this little issue that the place they just were, the womb, didn't have day or night, so they may get the two backwards. I'll get to remedies for that in a moment. Sleep periods at night will slowly get longer and longer. All of the sudden you'll get four hours of sleep and you'll feel like you had a month-long vacation.

Look at it from your baby's point of view. Imagine subsisting with a stomach the size of a walnut. Now imagine you're "on" every minute of the day. Everything you do and see is new, so you have to "process" everything. In fact, you have to learn how to process. Oh yeah, and you're on a liquid diet. You're going to get hungry…often. Guess what, when you're hungry you wake up. You can't speak, so when you're hungry you make the only noise you can, you cry. This, of course, is a different noise than an "ouch" or "frustrated" cry. Hopefully those big things that feed and change you will learn the difference before you get too upset and your "hungry" cry changes to an "ouch, I have gas" cry.

Call them myths, urban legends, or anecdotal information, but you will hear a lot about how to successfully get your baby to sleep through the night. For example, I was once told that at eleven pounds a baby has enough body mass to store enough energy to sleep through the night. It may be true, sometimes, but Ellie, our second child, grew to eleven pounds in about three weeks. Seven months later she was still not sleeping through the night. The bottom line is that every baby is different and they all develop at their own rate.

What do you do when you wake up in the middle of the night? Mumble something unintelligible? Go to the potty? (You'll start calling it that after you've had a child.) Go back to sleep? This is all learned behavior. Your baby doesn't know how to do any of that. She has to learn it. An important part of that is learning trust. Meaning she has to learn that no matter what, you'll be there for her. So when she wakes up in a dark room and realizes she's alone, she knows that if she cries out, you'll be there. With that knowledge, she'll sigh and go back to sleep. There is divergent research and opinion on the value of comforting versus "letting them cry it out." My opinion is that when you let your baby cry herself to sleep she is simply getting so worked up and exhausted that she falls asleep from sheer exhaustion. We chose to believe the research that shows that comforting a baby in the middle of the night teaches her trust and ultimately independence and self-reliance. We would go into the nursery, comfort the baby with soothing words and tell her to go back to sleep. It didn't work at first. We had to walk away, and she'd cry. Then we'd come back and do it again. Eventually she got to know we were there for her and learned how to comfort herself and go back to sleep. We can see the positive effect in all three of our very self-reliant kids.

As for the screen panels for the porch, we finally paid someone to rebuild them and learned not to take sleep for granted. Our kids all had extremely different sleep patterns. Sidney started sleeping thirteen hours a night at four months of age. Ellie slept all the time, about twenty hours a day, but only a few hours a time. She would not sleep through the night because she was growing so fast she would wake up hungry. This was very frustrating, not to mention exhausting and we started thinking about trying to get her back down without feeding her, or letting her work it out herself. Then we reread the sleep section in Dr. Sears' book. I'll paraphrase; expect your baby to be up twice a night between six and eight months, once a night between one and two years. The message: all babies are different (and may not get much sleep).

Learning Day and Night

"And days will become nights, and nights will become days." That's what our pediatrician told me the day Sidney was born. Because they have literally been in the dark for nine months babies may have the day and night thing backwards. You have to teach them what is day and what is night. To do this, during the day you should be active and playful and have bright colors and lively music. When evening sets in, change the music to lullabies. Dim the lights. Keep things quite. In about three days she should start to catch on to the whole day and night thing and get closer to your schedule. To be clear, babies are never really on your schedule, you're on theirs.

<u>Gas Relief via Swaddling</u>

Babies like tights spaces. Think about where they were for nine months. When your baby fusses, it is human nature to hold her tight. When she has gas, this may not be enough. Ask your doctor when it's safe to start giving her medicine for gas relief (see *Mylacon* in **Safety and First Aid**). In the meantime, you may want to try swaddling. Swaddling for gas relief is a method of tightly wrapping your baby in a blanket to give her relief from gas pain.

The first night of Sidney's life she had really bad gas. This is not unusual. Babies are suddenly thrust from the comfort of the womb to the outside world. Literally everything is new, especially breathing. In the womb babies get their air from the umbilical cord, so when the start to breathe on their own they tend to swallow a lot of air, which can give them gas. So there we were in the middle of the night bleary eyed and exhausted, oh and did I mention clueless, with a screaming child. We buzzed the night nurse, who came in, heard the pitch of the cry and said, "Oh, that's gas. Let me swaddle her." She wrapped Sidney tightly in a blanket and Sidney was instantly quiet. We took that lesson home. For the first two months, every time she had bad gas, we swaddled her tightly in a receiving blanket.

We called this "making a baby burrito." Here's how you do it:

Place a receiving blanket on the bed, square, not at an angle. Put your baby in the center of the top, with only her head sticking past the top of the blanket. Very firmly pull the corners over her shoulders at an angle covering and restricting her arms. Then fold the bottom up over her legs. The trick is to fold it tight enough for her knees to be drawn into her chest. Then fold the edges around her back so they stay in place. If, when you are making that last fold the blanket is over her head, double it over, so you're not suffocating your baby.

Apparently this position is very comforting for a newborn because it simulates the womb. Drawing the knees to the chest is also comforting if you have bad gas. Ever lie on the bed in the fetal position to help with a stomach ache? We were concerned that she wouldn't like being restricted like that, so we asked our doctor. He said if she didn't like it she'd kick the blanket off. And, indeed, Ellie did just that. The burrito trick was not nearly as effective with her, because she didn't want to be tightly swaddled.

Music and White Noise

A friend once told me to have our baby sleep in the noisiest room in the house. It was excellent advice. It may sound counter-intuitive, but the last thing you want is for your baby to only be able to fall and/or stay asleep when it's dead quite. Background noise is a fact of life. A perfect, albeit extreme, example of this occurred when Sidney was three months old. We were renovating the house and a construction crew came in at 7:30 am to tear out the subflooring in the attic above the nursery. To our horror we realized we had double-booked the construction crew and Sidney's sleep. The whole house was shaking, there was sawing, there was banging. Sidney slept like, you guessed it, a baby. There's still not much that will wake her when she's asleep.

Of course, you don't have to go to quite that length to teach your child to sleep when it's noisy. The simplest of these is to get a white noise machine. We found an inexpensive one that cost about twenty dollars. It made about five different sounds: ocean, rain, forest, heartbeat, and good old "white noise. You can also buy CDs with soothing ocean sounds or download an app to your iPhone or iPad.

Talk to Your Baby

I learned a surprising thing in one of those "how not to kill you baby" classes. The instructor asked us what we thought made children smart. What thing that parents do that had the same effect regardless of socio-economic status? The section heading give it away? That's right, talking to your baby, as soon as you can. Even in the womb. Talk about anything: your day, the weather, football. Tell him about it as you snap up his Onesie. Talk to him as often as you can. It can really make a difference in a child's life and it's one of the few things about raising child that doesn't have a price tag.

It's not a myth that your child will learn to recognize your voice when in utero. When Sandy was pregnant with Ellie I used to talk to her belly every night before bed. "I can't wait to meet you. Daddy loves you." Right after she was born and they put her on the warming table, she was fussing up a storm. Probably thinking: "What the hell am I doing here? How'd I get here? Who are you people?" Though it sounded strikingly like crying and screaming. I went over to her, leaned really close and said, "Hi, Ellie. Daddy's here. I love you." The crying stopped instantly! She calmed down because she recognized my voice. It was amazing. Let me rephrase that, it was AMAZING, goose bumps amazing.

<u>Music during Pregnancy</u>

Just like white noise, music can be soothing to your baby. This is true even before she's born. Just as your baby can recognize your voice if you speak to her in utero, so can she recognize music. Another lesson we learned by accident. When Sandy was pregnant with Sidney she had a long daily commute. She was hooked on the sound track to the movie *Shrek* and played it repeatedly. One day shortly after Sidney was born she was fussing and we were trying to calm her down by holding her, rocking her, and playing soothing music. The music ended and before we could do anything it switched to the next soundtrack, *Shrek*. Instantly she was quiet and calm. Definitely a mind-blowing experience as the first track of *Shrek* is not exactly a slow song. It was even more interesting to explain to my mother that it really was soothing and effective to rock her to sleep to "Bad Reputation" by Joan Jett.

Choose what you listen to during pregnancy carefully. You could be listening to it a lot, for a long time. I think Sidney was close to two when we could finally phase out *Shrek*. There's something gratifying to watching your toddler bounce up and down to "Bad Reputation" while she's strapped into her car seat. Or maybe we're just a little twisted, but you've got to work with what you've got.

<u>Singing</u>

There will be times that you won't have easy access to music, or white noise, or construction workers. It is important to have a portable means of soothing your baby and/or getting him to sleep. What better way than your own voice. At first you may be a little bashful. But eventually you'll get over it. Besides, people are used to seeing parents sing to their children. There's a reason why parents everywhere are goofy to the point of embarrassment: necessity. Even if you have a terrible voice, you'll sing. Your baby won't know you can't carry a tune. He'll be glad for the comfort.

As with the music you listen to during pregnancy, choose you songs well. You may be singing them for a long time. The ABC song is a particular favorite because it's entertaining, educational, and there are several derivatives in the form of "Twinkle, Twinkle" and "Bah, Bah, Black Sheep." Then came that fateful day when, between fourteen and eighteen month of age, our children realized that I was singing for the express purpose of putting them to sleep. The lower lip curled down and they'd start to cry and would say with their best manners, "Daddy, please stop singing." But then when they were tired and cranky and fussy they'd say, "Daddy, please sing me a song," which was music to my ears.

Flying and Boinging

Dads everywhere throw their kids in the air. Mom's everywhere gasp. If you do this when they are young, less than six months, be very careful, because their little necks can't support their little heads. So as an alternative to throwing her in the air I started "flying" Sidney. Basically, this started as holding her in the air over my head by her sides. Then pretending she was an airplane and flying her around in slow motion. Sandy was naturally a little concerned about the safety of this and checked with our doctor. He told us that as long as we are gentle there's no danger. In fact, he said, in some cultures they do this to their babies from an early age to get them ready to be gymnasts. I don't know if that's really true and you should check with your doctor about your specific acrobatics but the bottom line is Sidney loved to fly. Then Ellie did, then Calvin, then the cousins, etc. I'd run around the house buzzing the furniture and the dog. She'd shriek with joy, which would only encourage me. Sandy eventually got used to it. When I did it in public we'd forget it was not exactly typical and usually got a gasp from a nearby mother. Just make sure you're gentle and not shaking your baby too much. Shaken Baby Syndrome is very real and potentially harmful.

An alternative to flying is "boinging." This involved holding Baby by her sides under her armpits and gently bouncing her up and down as I walked. The key was to say "boing" each time her feet hit the ground. Because you're holding on firmly you can get some height and go horizontal off the wall, the dog, the counter, the door, chairs, tables, Grandpa. You name it. Sidney was invariably shrieking with joy and laughter. One word of caution, it can be very damaging to your child's shoulders if you lift and/or swing them by their arms. So flying, boinging, or swinging should be done while holding their bodies. And, remember, newborns must have their heads supported.

Kids Learn by Watching

I once saw an inspirational message outside a local church that has stuck with me. It read: "Just remember, every day you are teaching your children how to raise their children." True that! There's no doubt our children learn by watching what we do. Sidney would pick up the "bugle" from the breast pump, pull up her shirt, and put in on her chest. She didn't know what she was doing, but she saw Mommy do it every morning. She'd try to brush her hair, because that's what we did. Granted she held the bush with the bristles up and brushed up instead of down, but to her, she was following our example. So goes it with virtually everything you say and do. You'll come to realize there are things you never realized you did until your child starts doing them. For example, Sidney started saying "okay" at the end of almost every sentence. We wondered where she learned it. Then someone pointed out that at the end of virtually every question we asked her we said, "okay?" at the end. A lot of it is cute, but there are things that you might not want to hear your two year old say, so be careful.

Teaching Love and Respect

One of the many things we strive to teach our kids is love and respect. Okay, that's two things, but they go together. Since kids have to be taught virtually everything, we feel it's important to focus them on loving and respecting each other, their parents, other people, the environment, the dog, you name it. There is no shortage of teaching moments with this. When Calvin hit one of his friends the other day we pulled him aside and talked to him about it. We asked him what was going on, why he did it, etc. Of course the answer we got was a shrug, because he was too young to articulate, but when we asked him if it was "okay" he knew the answer. We've spent countless hours on "use you words." If Ellie acts out, we point out that her behavior is showing other people how she wants to be treated. "Do you want people to grab your toys?" The golden rule sinks in faster when it's done real-time.

And nothing warms our hearts more than watching the kids give each other morning hugs. They learned this from us because our day always starts with a hug. But to see them reciprocate with each other is a wonderful thing. If one of the other kids isn't feeling well or is hurt, Sidney instantly is protective. To me it just underlines that hatred is learned behavior. If we choose not to teach it, perhaps the world will become a better place.

Chapter Nineteen - Commentary on Life – Stuff About You

A guy I work with likes to start sentences with "no offense, but…" and then drop a bomb. I love it. I never have to guess what he really thinks. So, no offense, but you're crazy if you don't think that everything in your life changes when you have a child: the center of your world, your car, maybe your health, and your relationship with your partner. When all is said and done, however, modeling a healthy relationship is one of the best things you can do for your child. It goes right along with "they learn by watching," and if you want them to grow up and have a happy, healthy marriage, it starts with what you model to them. So here are some life lessons that I feel I should pass along.

The Importance of Keeping in Shape

When I was a young(er) man I was very active. But things changed and I stacked off and at thirty-five it was a long road back to fitness. I think my first "run" was about a quarter mile. But I kept with it and eventually got to a more respectable three to five miles. Since then I have stayed in decent shape. Sandy also stays quite fit, which is one of the things that drew us together.

The point is that a baby, who turns into a toddler, who never runs out of energy, doesn't understand the concept of age nor the concept of Daddy (or Mommy) being tired. Children want to play. My father-in-law says that now that he has grandchildren he understands why children are meant for the young. My opinion is that no matter how old you are it's important to keep in shape. I was thirty-nine when we had our first baby. Everything you do with your child is an opportunity to teach, and active play is no exception. Rolling around with your infant on the floor may not be "exercise," but it takes energy. Then once he starts to crawl and pull himself up on things you'll be running around behind him to be nearby for the inevitable times he falls over. Too many head bangs are bad. Once he starts to walk, you're running even more. All of this takes energy. Energy you won't have if you're not in shape.

Being is shape lets me give my children the best childhood I can. So, no offense, but get in shape as early as you can, before you have kids, if possible. Then when they're small you can maintain your condition. Maybe even keep up with them.

Staying in shape once the baby is born is a whole different ballgame. You're tired all the time and you don't seem to have any time for anything but Baby and sleep. After three months things may start to calm down and you may have some workout time. When our kids were very young and we had limited time I did my best to maintain my physical condition so that once the kids were a little older I wasn't starting all over. It's a long road back to fitness that gets longer the older you get. Here are some things that worked for us.

- We took turns going to the gym or getting in a short run.
- Sandy would to get in a quick run during the week when a babysitter or neighbor was at the house.
- We had a neighbor who would occasionally watch the girls so we could get in a run together (a real treat as long as I didn't mind getting left in the dust.)
- I always get in a workout when I travel.
- We got a jogging stroller (see *Strollers* in **Getting Around**) so we could take the kids with us on our runs.

In our society, with so many people overweight, we should do everything we can to teach our kids to exercise. By exercising while she was pregnant Sandy thinks (and read) that the kids will have a natural tendency to exercise because their bodies will already be used to the endorphins secreted while exercising. We all have it in our power to break the chain of inactivity. The more you exercise, the more your children will. Exercise is therefore a central part of our lives. When the kids got to school age they were required to have one activity each semester that kept them moving. It could be dance or soccer or swimming, but they got plenty of exercise. By teaching our kids the importance of exercise we are giving them a richer, longer future.

A Word about Minivans (the "M" Word)

Your mode of transportation with your children and your family is a personal choice. We swore we would never get a minivan, AKA the "M" word. I think it's one of the reasons I married Sandy. They were for, well, other people. There are a lot of alternatives out there and, depending on your family size, you may not need to drive a minivan. It took us a while to eventually break down and get a minivan, but consider this: it seems that most families get a minivan. There's a reason for that. But if you are only planning on having one child, and you have a car that's safe, there's no reason to go out and buy something bigger. Unless you're traveling with a dog, and/or you're a terrible packer, you'll be fine in a sedan. And for many people, an SUV or station wagon is all they need.

When we started planning a future that would include kids we decided to get a mid-sized SUV so we'd have room for three kids, the dog, and all our stuff. We quickly learned that since the dog needed half the cargo space and there wasn't enough width to install three car seats in one row that we'd always be using a car-top carrier on long trips. If we had only wanted, or had, two kids we may still have an SUV, but with three it became impractical for us. Sandy tested a minivan by accident having stepped into a friend's to nurse Ellie. There was ample room for her, and more important there was a passage between the two front seats giving the adults easy access to the kids. We did a lot of research on safety through *Consumer Reports* and the National Transportation Safety Board (NTSB) to assuage our safety concerns about rear impact. Minivans today have a wide variety of options including navigation systems, built-in movie players, and large, powerful engines. It seems the manufacturer's market research people got it right. The mileage is not as good as a sedan, but generally better than the super-large "land yacht" SUVs.

Why You Should Get a Dog

Sandy and I are dog people. Throughout both our childhoods we had a family dog. So now our kids are dog people. They ride her; jump on her; throw her a ball, a stick, a Frisbee. We wanted a dog for companionship, but there's one major benefit to having a dog that never occurred to us: cleaning. Some 52% of all baby food ends up on the ground. (This is based on my extremely scientific statistical research: personal observation.) This is particularly true between the ages of eight months and two years when having a well-trained dog around is priceless. When we're traveling we really miss our yellow Lab, Sophie. There's so much more to clean up! We also realized that Sophie put on a lot of weight clearing the table for us. I'm not kidding. She would take the plates, one at a time, to the door mat where they wouldn't "clink" when she put them down, and lick them clean. When we finally caught on that "no" wasn't working, she gave us these dirty looks every time we cleared the table. Sophie even cleaned up the post-burp spit up that's inevitable. (Don't criticize. All I had to do was say "here girl" and that splot would be gone and the dog got a treat.)

Dogs aren't for everyone. And you have to make sure you get one with the right temperament. There's plenty of research out there praising the value of having cats and/or dogs. For example, petting them may lower your blood pressure, they're great companions, and they teach kids about responsibility. There's even research that shows early exposure to cats and dogs may reduce pet allergies later in life. Because we both had dogs growing up, after we got married, but before we had kids, we decided to get a dog. It went more like, I wanted a dog and Sandy was concerned about having one and starting a family. But we did some research (surprise) and for Christmas Sandy got me a Lab puppy.

Having any animal is a commitment. If you decide to get a dog before or after you have children, the issues you have to consider and overcome are finding the right breed, as some dogs are not baby friendly, and training. You can do your own research about breeds on the American Kennel Club website, www.akc.org or take on online quiz at www.selectsmart.com/DOG/ or animal.discovery.com/breed-selector/dog-breeds.html. Generally, Labrador Retrievers (yellow or black) and Golden Retrievers are great with kids.

Training falls into three categories: puppy preschool, command training, and getting ready for Baby. Puppy preschool started the day we brought Sophie home. We had our fingers in her food when she ate, so she learned that her food was fair game. In fact she couldn't ever start to eat until released with an "okay." We poked her, gently pulled her ears, her tail. Kids will be all over a dog, or cat, so make sure you teach them (the animal, not the kid) not to overreact to the tail-pulling and eye-poking they're sure to get from your child. We (Sandy) spent countless hours teaching Sophie not to play bite, not to chew on toys and furniture, not to jump on people, etc. We also learned that since they don't have arms, dogs don't understand hugging. It's the first thing a three year old will likely do, so hugging was part of "preschool." Sophie's a champ. You can do anything to her, including take food out of her mouth.

Command training starts when your puppy is about four to six months old. You teach things like: "come," "stay," "sit." We worked with a professional trainer and used the leash correction method. There are other methods that may seem less harsh. You can do it all yourself, work from a book about training, hire a trainer to come to your house, or you can send your puppy to training school. Either way, training is a commitment. But having a well-trained dog is an important way to ensure that you don't lose your sanity and that your kids and property don't get hurt.

To get ready for Baby, you need to train your dog (or cat), old or young, that there will be a new member of the household. Animals can be a little territorial and protective. Once your baby is born it's a good idea to bring home a Onesie or a hat from the hospital that Baby has been wearing. Let the dog sniff it and speak in soothing tones. That way the dog will get used to the smell and it won't be a new thing when you bring the baby home. Under no circumstances should you let the dog use the hat or Onesie as a toy. For more information about this see *Hats* in the **Clothing** section. (Yes "Hats," not "cats." You'll understand when you read it.)

Time for the Two of You, Keeping the Romance

One of the first things that you'll notice after you have a baby, after you get used to being completely exhausted, is that you and your wife aren't spending as much quality time together. During those first few months the baby needs you all the time, you're tired, exhausted actually, and you basically meet up in bed each night, mumble "I love you," and get your two hours of sleep before the baby wakes you up again. Your wife is also healing. It will take four to eight weeks for her body to get back to normal. After about three months, the haze starts to lift. It's really important that at this time you start to schedule some time for the two of you. I am not suggesting that you neglect your child. I am simply saying you shouldn't neglect your relationship with your wife. Gone are the days you can up and go to dinner and a movie. In fact, once we started getting a babysitter to watch Sidney, we'd get as far as dinner before Sandy missed her so much that we'd have to turn around and go home. But we slowly started to work in a little more time for each other. She is the woman I love, ridiculous amounts, and I want to have some time alone with her when we're not both exhausted. I thought at the time that we'd have to wait till the kids were in their teens to get away for the weekend. In reality, we worked our way into longer periods of alone time starting with romantic evenings or the quiet walks. We got help from babysitters and/or Grandma watching the kids. Once the youngest was about two, we were able to get away for a long weekend. You have to do what feels right for you.

Finding a Good Babysitter

To be able to do anything independent of your child you'll need good babysitters. Whether it's going to the movies or a school board meeting you're going to have some times when you're both busy and someone else needs to watch your children. Some people are fortunate enough to live close to a loving family that is willing to watch their nieces, nephews, or grandchildren just about any time. The rest of us have to develop a babysitter pool. This is easier said than done. After two years we only had two or three, outside of family, that we trusted.

Good babysitters are hard to come by. This is especially true when the children are infants, as the care is so much more involved. And once you find one you won't want to tell your friends about her because you won't want to risk having her busy on that Saturday night you want her. That said, we found it was generally word of mouth that led us to a babysitter. We worked our way into our early babysitters by having them come over and watch the girls while we were at the house. We'd have her play with them in another room and, well, eavesdrop. If you're happy with what you hear, leave the house for an hour or so. Eventually you'll establish some trust. It's a constant dilemma and there's no reason you can't start looking before you have your baby (except for that whole coming over and watching her while you're home thing). By the time your child gets to school age you'll have a lot of practice finding sitters and it won't seem so daunting. Still, there are some events we have had to skip because we couldn't find help. There is also something to be said for the "it takes a village" approach of being able to rely on your neighbors in a pinch. For example, sometimes we'd swap childcare. Meaning "You watch mine Wednesday and I'll watch yours Friday." After a while arranging for care becomes second nature, but getting going can be a challenge.

When Sandy went back to work we looked for a nanny by advertising online. If you do this, expect a lengthy screening process. Once you land on someone you like, check some references. They all should be glowing. We are also fortunate that the Parent Teacher Organization at our kids' school publishes, as part of the parent contact directory, a list of middle school kids who want to babysit. Gold mine! This was fine for the occasional afternoon but when we needed someone older, who could ferry the kids to their activities one day a week, Sandy got online at www.sittercity.com. You have to pay a monthly fee to join, but they do all the screenings and background checks. We still interviewed the candidates, but it was much less painful than our earlier foray when we did the advertising ourselves.

Laughter, Hugs and Kisses

A child's laugh is one of the most glorious sounds in the universe. Once your baby can laugh, spend all the time you can learning new ways to get her to laugh. It's a great way to interact, stimulate, and get to know her. All of your problems go away when she laughs at you.

Next she'll be able to put her little arms around your neck and hug you. I think melt is the best word for what it does to you. So tiny, yet such a firm touch.

Then one day she'll learn how to kiss you. "May I please have a kiss?" I'd ask Sidney and was rewarded by a gentle, wet peck on the cheek. "And a hug too," she'd say. Life truly is good!

And then out of the blue, she'd say, "I love you, Daddy." Perhaps there are better things in life, but on that day, it was the best thing that's ever happened.

The Last Stuff

When we had our first baby, Sidney, we were overwhelmed, and to a great degree unprepared for the amount of stuff we would need. Fortunately, you really don't need it all at once. Our midwife told us right after our second child, Ellie, was born that when we got her home everything would seem easy and we'd wonder why it was so hard the first time. She was right. And although there's no substitute for experience, hopefully some of the things put forth here will help you be better prepared. This book started out as a simple list for my brother. When I began writing it I realized that a list wasn't enough because there was a story behind almost every decision we made. My hope is that these stories will help you put things into perspective when making your choices.

We are exposed every day to the choices people make and, I'm sure, have an opinion about them. Remember, there's no accounting for taste. What you like is personal and for you to decide. You have to make your own choices, about stuff, and about parenting. In the end there is no one right answer.

There is no greater reward than watching your child grow. Bill Murray said in the movie *Lost in Translation* that having your first baby is terrifying "but then they learn how to walk, and they learn to how to talk, and you want to be with them. And then they turn out to be the most delightful people you will ever meet in your life." How true!

Cheers,

JG

About the Author

In addition to learning about life with children, Jed Gibson has grown accustomed to the bedlam of parenthood with his extended family of four in-laws and seven nieces and nephews. Often referred to as Uncle Daddy, he puts to use all of his skills as a carpenter, architect, chief cook, and bottle washer. Raised in a quiet New York suburb, he now resides outside of Philadelphia with his wife, three kids, and a dog.

www.ingramcontent.com/pod-product-compliance
Lightning Source LLC
LaVergne TN
LVHW051508080426
835509LV00017B/1973